PRAISE FOR DEBRA KEYES
AND THE S.P.I.C.E. OF LIFE

For better than two decades, I have witnessed Debra Keyes embrace both professional and personal challenges as opportunities for emotional, spiritual, and physical growth and success. She is a living witness to the power of tenacity, spirit, and faith. She does not hide her light under a bushel basket. Rather, her light shines, that others may experience their own light.

> **REV. FR. DOUGLAS A. GREENAWAY**, *President and CEO, National WIC Association*

Debra Keyes epitomizes the integrity, engagement, and wealth of knowledge sorely needed in our communities today. *The S.P.I.C.E. of Life* is compelling, inspiring, and a great resource for raising self-awareness, sharing a range of lived experiences, action planning to go forward in life, and giving back to one's community and society.

> **DR. ELAINE PARKER-GILLS**, *Education Coordinator, Career Build Community, Inc.*

The S.P.I.C.E. of Life is an amazingly written book that guides you through living a whole and prosperous life. It gives you the opportunity to apply concepts to your life regardless of your own spiritual beliefs and personal habits.

> **MERCEDES JOHNSON**, *CEO, JMP Consulting Group*

The S.P.I.C.E. of Life offers a feast of Light for our personal growth and healing.

> **KAMAU DAAOOD**, *Performance Poet*

more…

I know her story. I was there for many of the ups and downs. I bore witness to the transformation. She has led by example and taught me many life lessons. She is my mother. Now the time has come for the world to receive some of this wisdom!

TALIB HAMILTON, *Entrepreneur*

This book reveals the depth of Debra's journey through this life. How generous and bold of her to share her innermost self with those who dare to desire their own transformation.

REV. ERROLL PARKER, *Christian Minister*

After hearing Debra Keyes's presentation, I must say she was outstanding. I had no idea of her spiritual gift. I pray she continues to give as God has given to her.

BISHOP DR. BARBARA LEWIS KING, *World Spiritual Leader and Founder, Hillside International Truth Center*

Debra Keyes does a phenomenal job in simplifying the best ways to get the most out of our lives. She is loving, engaging, and humorous. This book should be read by all!

DR. ADOLPH BROWN III, *Author, Master Teacher, and Social Justice Advocate*

Debra Keyes is living in her truth and sharing it with others in The S.P.I.C.E. of Life, a teaching memoir. She is honest, encouraging, forward-thinking, and motivational with her ideas and her passion for healthy living. With her knowledge and experiences, she provides a trail map for others to follow positively through their own transformations of life.

DR. THURMA M. GOLDMAN, MPH, *US Public Health Service (retired)*

THE SPICE
OF LIFE

Key Ingredients for Transformative Living

DEBRA L. KEYES

LEAD*right*

Atlanta, Georgia

Disclaimer: The contents of The S.P.I.C.E. of Life: Key Ingredients for Transformative Living are for informational purposes only. The content is not intended to be a substitute for professional advice, diagnosis, or treatment. Always seek the advice of your health professional or other qualified health provider with any questions, concerns, observations, or insights you may have regarding your health and wellness. Never disregard professional advice or delay in seeking it because of something you have read in The S.P.I.C.E. of Life: Key Ingredients for Transformative Living.

The events, locales, and conversations in this book are portrayed to the best of Debra's memory. In order to maintain the anonymity of some people, she has changed or omitted the names of individuals and places in some instances. She has also changed some identifying characteristics and details such as physical properties, occupations, and places of residence. The conversations in this book all come from her recollections. Though they are not written to represent word-for-word transcripts, she has retold them in a way that evokes the feeling and meaning of what was said and, in all instances, the essence of the dialogue is accurate. This is Debra's story; those who disagree with her truth, as shared in this book, are invited to write their own.

Cover Concept by Talib H. Hamilton
Cover Design and Chapter Graphics by www.justrawcreatives.com
Back Cover Photo by Seven Jackson
Formatting and Indexing by LEADright
Copyediting by Richard Allen

Printed and bound in the United States of America

The S.P.I.C.E. of Life: Key Ingredients for Transformative Living [a teaching memoir] / Debra L. Keyes — 1st ed.

ISBN 978-1-954556-20-1

DEDICATION

My Angels: My parents, Delores and Luther; my sister, Kathi; my grandmothers, Edith and Ida; my spiritual sister, Layona; Aunt Linda; Grandma Betty; Cousin Cheri; and my spiritual leaders, Rev. Juanita Dunn, Dr. Dan L. Morgan, and Dr. Barbara Lewis King.

My Personal Board of Directors: My Brother, BaBa Kamau; my spiritual sister, Debra Ward; my mentor and adopted family, Dr. Adolph Brown III; and my spiritual mothers, Gladys Hudson and Rev. Gertrude Moore.

My Life Force: My one and only son, Talib Hamilton I, and my grandson, Talib Hamilton II.

CONTENTS

PREFACE

On a clear day, rise and look around you,
and you'll see who you are.
from the musical,
"On a Clear Day (You Can See Forever)"
by Burton Lane and Alan Jay Lerner

AWARENESS BUILDS CLARITY ™

I can hear her now. My beautiful mother, the singer who left her singing dreams behind to raise, nurture, and love her family. She always exposed us to the best way to live our lives–even as young children–either through her words or just in the way she lived her life. She was a woman of grace and integrity. Everything that I needed to know to survive life's journey was given to me by my Mama. My mama used to sing this song, a favorite of hers. She may not have even known how profound and enlightening the lyrics were. In "Clarity," you can see forever and ever more.

This book was inspired by my own journey through life. I am you; we are one. We all have a story to tell. In telling my stories, you may find pieces of yourself. I trust you will relate to my experiences. This is all part of a journey to embrace the S.P.I.C.E. of life that will transform you now and forever.

I have lived a long life. I am in my mid-60s at the time of this writing. Will there be another 50 years? Who knows. I have spent this first half of my life living for others, and I am now looking forward to decades more living life for me.

I have had many ups and downs, much like anyone else. I often did not heed the warning signs flashing right in front of me throughout my life. The warnings often were wake-up calls. If I had listened to them, perhaps they would have resulted in me living a different "best" life. Maybe I could have avoided a few pitfalls along the way.

Interestingly enough, my original title for this book was *Final Warning*. People often miss or ignore the warning signs—what I now call "Blessings in Disguise"—that are right in front of us. We miss these warnings because our focus is on everyone and everything else. Instead of living the awesome life created for us, we live for others. We may do this because perhaps we don't have a clue how wonderful we are as individuals.

Final Warning felt heavy. I want to uplift others and not sound the doom and gloom alarm. So I took time to reflect and rethink. I desired something life-affirming and positive. We are learning many lessons in our lifetime. We can beat the odds. We can grow, survive, thrive, and flourish if we have clarity. I knew I needed to spice my title up. I felt compelled to convey this truth: regardless of our pasts, our origins, and starts, or where we are today, it is never too late to embrace the "S.P.I.C.E. of Life." Now, how does that sound? Wouldn't you say this resonates deep down? Doesn't it give a more uplifting and inspirational feeling? The stories I tell and the insights I offer are told in truth. They are hard lessons learned. They are tips and suggestions that may provide insights on living and bringing the S.P.I.C.E. to—or back to—your life.

What does it mean to embrace the "S.P.I.C.E. of Life"?

It means awakening ourselves from our dormant state of being. It means revealing your perfect authentic self. It means showing up in pure and genuine ways. It means being the original you. The "YOU" you.

Most of us strive for perfection. As a young child, my mother always told me that "one can only do one's best." Live your best life, be your best self. One thing for sure, we all come to this place, this life, with a purpose. WHAT IS THAT PURPOSE? We struggle to understand that purpose. We search and search and often think we have found it. We live our lives doing what we THINK or BELIEVE our purpose in life is to be. Even if it does not feel right, we think we are on the right path. We do what we think is for our best good. Are we doing so because someone else told us, "you are perfect for this, or you are great at that"? We do it, and it makes us feel good, for a while, but often only for a while. Then we think, "maybe, this is not my purpose; maybe I should be doing something other than what I am doing." We might go through our whole life unfulfilled and feeling lost, feeling disconnected. In TRUTH, we are never lost.

At times many of us are unaware of who we are. We may not take time to listen and hear that "Still Small Voice" that comes from a bigger Source. We may not devote time to listening for the voice that speaks to us daily. We may ignore the voice that says, "Take a moment each day to take a breath and take it all in. Your answers will come."

There are many paths one can travel to become clear. There are many tools, tips, and tasks that we pick up along our journey through life that are valuable and necessary. My mantra in life is "Awareness Builds Clarity." It is as easy as ABC, as simple as 123 (ok, I just channeled the Jacksons!).

Nothing happens in life by mistake. And if you believe that and really know this to be true, you will never have a worry in life. You may always ask, "What is my lesson or my blessing in this situation?" You will always know it is for your highest and best good. You may feel anxious to know the answer; but, you will not worry. You will always carry that sense of peace. Because deep down inside, you will know your Truth.

This book was Divinely birthed through me as a way of cultivating awareness to build clarity. Living a Transformative Life, what a Blessing! This means living a life that is open and receptive to change and to shifts in order to live our most beautiful lives.

Debra L. Keyes
Atlanta, Georgia
December 2021

ACKNOWLEDGMENTS

I have a flood of gratitude in my heart for so many who have contributed to my life and to where I am today. Being able to write a book like this is only possible after living this journey personally and having so many loving family members, friends, mentors, and supporters.

First and foremost, I acknowledge my parents, Luther and Delores Keyes. They both shaped the person I am and have become. They did so, each in their own unique ways: Daddy with his no-nonsense, "you can do better" message to me. No matter how well I did or how good I looked, he was a man of little encouraging words and would often say, "you can do better." My mama's message to me was, "one can only do their best." She always showed her delight in me and all that I did. Over the years, I understood how each style was what shaped me today. To see and know me is to know Luther and Delores. Daddy gave me the balls, and mama gave me the heart. And I am driven by both of those attributes. Mama gave me my sensitive side, and daddy gave me my hard core. I know I can do better, even when I have doubted myself. Both gave me unconditional love. Agape LOVE. I felt it then, and I still feel it today. May they continue to Rest in Eternal Peace and Heaven.

Thank you to my son Talib, who literally saved my life. Admittedly, this was a very hard core burden to put on a little life; it became one he has carried through his life. He may not feel that way, but it is what it is. To him, I apologize as I also thank him. He was born the day before my mama, my life, made her transition. What was there to live for? I could not imagine life without her. The new life, my new responsibility, my son, was my savior. I thank his father for having that reason or season to be in my life. No, it was not for a lifetime, but he gifted me with the best gift of all.

Thank you to my one and only grandchild, Talib ll. He is the joy and the strength of my life. He experienced tragedy at an early age of this life; his mother made her transition. Because he embodied the strength of his ancestors, he is our rock. I call him "The Mini Ta," just like his dad. He is a beautiful human being and is destined to be the GOAT in whatever he endeavors to do or be. His trajectory: "The Sky's the Limit."

A special Thank you to my siblings. My big brother, Kamau. The griot and poet. My protector and role model, living his life sharing his God-given gifts and talents. Kathi, my beloved sister, gone much too soon. She was affectionately known as Aisha, meaning LIFE. Her infectious laugh and silly spirit stay with me, and I draw from her spirit every day. To all of my true friends, way too many to name. I am Blessed because of you.

Thank you to my team of book reviewers and cheering squad—Talib Hamilton, Debra Ward, Thurma Goldman, Lynn Flen, Camille Cowans, Theresa Whitaker, and Ashaki Evens. I appreciate your candid comments that have made this a better book. I also wish to thank my absolutely wonderful writing coach, Dr. Tony Lamair Burks II, for his support, patience, and encouragement with my first book.

INTRODUCTION

THE SPICE OF LIFE provides insights, tools, and remedies to awaken the spirit and inspire transformative living through five elements:

Spirituality
Personal Growth and Development
Introspection
Conscious Connection
Energy Management

This book is as much about you as it is about me. *THE S.P.I.C.E. OF LIFE: Key Ingredients for Transformative Living*–on the one hand–tells the story of how balancing SPICE transformed my life. On the other hand, its purpose is to allow you–as the reader–to examine each element of your life. I want you to consider how important each element is in your life. You'll see what an element looks like now and where you would like to see it in the near future. There will be stories told and tools and tips shared. Each chapter provides an opportunity for you to reflect on the lessons learned. You will have space to write your personal story on the topic. I invite you to examine each element of SPICE to determine how these attributes are manifesting and developing in your life. Then we'll focus on how to bring them into an ideal balance.

We know from experience that success in any endeavor seems to demand a "Singleness of Purpose." To succeed, we need to focus on that one thing and give it "our all." We falter when we are not focused. When we are scattered, we end up going in all directions and getting nowhere. The question is, "What is it to which we should give 'our all'"?

Certainly, we know that if work is the most important thing, it's unhealthy. If you are ignoring your health or your family, it's both unhealthy and can be disastrous. It can be the same if religion or your social community is the priority. If family is first–to the exclusion of your own well-being–that's also counterproductive.

The one thing that promises to deliver balance is to make wholeness the singular focus and goal. "Whole," in relation to our lives, represents more than the health of the body. Wholeness is about the health of the psyche, mind, and spirit. Such wholeness is in harmony with existence itself. Your spirit is one with the spirit of life. All of this works together as a single undiversified whole unit for life.

You will notice that the categories in the acronym S.P.I.C.E. are suggestions. They are customizable and specific to the person. You may desire other categories that resonate more with your needs and desires and with your life journey. You may like to get an understanding of areas such as "Society." Perhaps you may want to have "Family and Friends" or "Romance" as separate categories. I invite you to deeply explore whatever areas are true for you. You will come to understand as you read this how you can choose your path or categories. Use whatever information comes up in your spirit or in your gut. Then focus on adjusting these areas to bring the desired SPICE to your life.

The SPICE of YOUR Life!–from Spirituality and Personal

Growth and Development to Introspection, Conscious Connections, and Energy Management—looks at attributes manifesting and developing in my life. These attributes are more than simply pieces of a pie representing a percentage of time in my life. For me, they are constantly occurring in my daily existence. They are the circumference of our being. They are with us 24 hours a day, 7 days a week, 365 days a year. They must become something we are and do unconsciously. Keep this in your conscious mind. Have you heard of *The Wheel of Life?* Many of us learned about it because of our work in life coaching, business coaching, and personal development. *The Wheel of Life* is a tool, a circle, divided into sections that represent areas of your life. It suggests that there must be an equal share of the pie for you to survive and strive.

I was exposed to *The Wheel of Life* during a workshop. At the time, I felt my life was all over the place, feeling successful in some areas of life but failing in others. I had to get my life in balance; otherwise, I was a failure: as a mother, a mate, an employee, a true friend, and on and on. The workshop where I learned about *The Wheel of Life* was great because I learned I was living an out-of-balance life. This awareness built clarity, and I started my journey to bring balance to my world. Though helpful for where I was at the time, working to make the parts of the wheel in the pie split evenly. This did not make sense to me. I was just not the right person for it. *The Wheel of Life* was a great discovery, but there must be more to this concept.

The Wheel of Life, as a concept, requires us to separate our life into slivers that never truly seem to be enough. I see *The Wheel of Life* concept differently. Through the years, there have been many approaches one can use to balance life or "even out" life activities. Truthfully, that is somewhat impossible. And you really wouldn't want everything to be evenly distributed; you cannot make everything even. Think about Life. It is all constantly moving parts that must be included at different times or even at the same time in different stages of one's life. I kept thinking about *The Wheel of Life* and what was essential to help me on my journey.

Eventually, I thought about *Maslow's Hierarchy of Needs*, a very popular framework of life and living represented as a pyramid with the most basic needs at the bottom. This theory comprises five tiers or levels that we all must go through in our lives. It is a pyramid of human needs. This philosophy encourages people to obtain and research information, tips, suggestions, and inspirational insights that will enable individuals to unleash their true selves and live a fulfilled life. The goal here is to reach self-actualization.

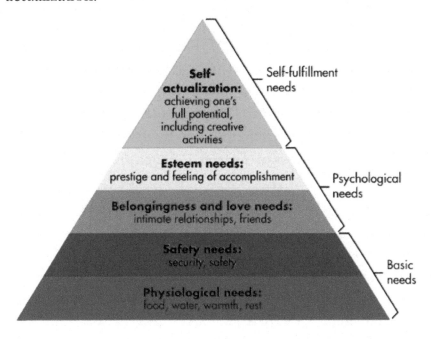

Maslow's Hierarchy of Needs

In this context, I am referring to the top of the tier, our ultimate goal in this life—self-actualization, self-fulfillment. We all search to achieve our full potential and to serve our purpose in this life. Although all stages must be met to achieve this level, we are all at certain points on this journey. There are those who feel that they are on track, while there are many that feel we are off track.

For many, it takes time; in my case, it took years and years. It is such a blessing to be here. It is never too late to begin your journey to self-actualization. To live your purpose to be your authentic self. We have to go-through what we go-through in life. Actually, let me expand that: "We have to GROW-through what we GO-through in life in order to receive the message and make whatever necessary transformations we need to make."

Trust me; once you receive that final warning, you are now ready, open, and receptive. These warnings come to us in many ways and through many life experiences. At this point, you have no choice. Yes, it would be better if you do not have to reach the point of a final warning; however, let's be truthful, most of us have to reach that point.

A WORD ABOUT THE SPICE OF LIFE WHEEL™ KEY INGREDIENTS

The SPICE of Life Wheel™, as a divine idea, takes what I learned from *The Wheel of Life, Maslow's Hierarchy of Needs,* and my lived experiences then offer a concept and perspective that is realistic and attainable. *The SPICE of Life Wheel™* in this book moves us from traditional wheels and hierarchies to concepts that bring fulfillment and excitement to our lives, our world, and our affairs.

The SPICE of Life Wheel ™ has two essential aspects. The first essential aspect is your circumference. This is your outer protection; it is the coat of armor. It is constant and steadfast in our lives. The key message is that "YOUR" SPICE is changeless and is always present. It is never divided or sliced. It cements and holds us together. It is a must for your life. Your circumference will differ from mine. What is important is that it is all about what works for you. The second essential aspect is all about how you express yourself and fully engage in your life's journey. While the circumference or the outer is changeless, the inner is about how you devote yourself to what makes life fulfilling. It will change as you slice and divide things to your desire. This is where you determine how much time and energy you will devote to certain areas of your life.

Here's the idea: Once you've finished a chapter–or the whole book–take a moment to explore the *Menu of Possibilities* located in the Extra Ingredients section at the end of the book to brainstorm your specific areas of focus —the inward stuff. For example, after completing the brainstorming process, you decide to focus on "Nutrition." This means for the next 20 to 40 days, you would invest in examining and transforming your nutrition using S.P.I.C.E. (that is, Spirituality, Personal Growth and Development, Introspection, Conscious Connections, and Energy Management). Or maybe after brainstorming, you have multiple foci and wish to look at S.P.I.C.E. in four areas; let's say, Religion, Leisure Time, Finances, and Family. In this case, you might devote the next 20 to 60 days to working on all four areas at the same time. Or perhaps, you might work on each area for 15 days—one right after the other. Whatever you decide, I strongly encourage you to invest at least 15 days in an area of focus. Your transformation is worth every minute!

There are many ways to get the most out of this book. You can read the chapters in order, completing the exercises along the way. You can flip to whatever chapter resonates in your soul and start there. You could even start with one of the exercises and then read a chapter. What matters most is that you are engaging in your transformation through Spirituality, Personal Growth and

Development, Introspection, Conscious Connections, and Energy Management.

I've formatted this book with purpose and intention: My desire is for it to be practical and useful to you; after all, "Keeping It Simple" is what we all desire. For instance, the ABCs were one of the easiest things I learned in grade school. You will find that I've adopted the ABC approach throughout this book. The point of it all is to help you follow the tips and tools with ease and be able to recall them when you need them during your day-to-day living.

As Benjamin Franklin often shared (and I paraphrase), if you tell them they will forget, if you show them they may remember; but, if you involve them, they will learn and embody. I encourage you to jump into each chapter with two feet. My desire is to fully involve and engage you in your own growth process. When you do it this way, things "stick," and there is typically a long-lasting, positive effect.

Although I share a few personal stories along the way, this book is as much about you as it is about me. In fact, *The SPICE of Life* book and wheel are all about YOU. Are you ready to get started? Great! I have a question for you: How do you eat a pie? Really, how do you do it? You eat it one slice at a time!

A NOTE ABOUT WRITING AND REFLECTING

It seems that each month, I meet a few people who say to me, "I've always wanted to write a book!" Well, guess what? If you read *The SPICE of Life* and complete the exercises, self-work, and self-reflections, you will have completed the first draft manuscript of your memoir, your story, your book! Like me, you have a story to tell. Whether your writing benefits others, remains locked in your computer, or for your own reflective practice, writing and storytelling are healing, and they strengthen your own soul. If you want to learn more about the process I went through to bring the book you're holding in your hands to life, check out the Extra Ingredients in the back of this book.

Spirituality

SPIRITUALITY

Spirituality, for me, is the Number One driving force for life. I see it now as the cocoon that has always guarded, protected, directed, and guided my life's journey. It is the force in the universe that constantly and consistently envelops, surrounds, and embraces us in a protective and comforting way. As a young child, I struggled with understanding God. I knew at a young age that there was a higher power. And people would tell us there was a big man in the sky. I had a unique understanding of God and how God worked in my life, even as a child. My parents, as I came to know, believed in God but were inconsistent churchgoers. Mama tried to raise us in the church, but my daddy did not want any part of the church. The story is, daddy's mother raised her family in the church, and as a young child, my dad witnessed something. I think, perhaps, the minister made advances toward his mother. She was widowed, and my dad was very protective of her. One Sunday during church, the minister called her out or said something about my grandmother that was unkind. After this occurred, my dad had a bad feeling about the church and the minister. In fact, he felt the minister was a hypocrite because my Dad witnessed him being a womanizer. He never trusted churches and especially the ministers, and never went to church. Because of this, I grew up somewhat confused about religion, church, and God. Mommie wanted to raise us in the church, and Daddy did not care about it for himself. He did not keep us from attending church and developing our own understanding of religion and spirituality.

In 1972, I was 19 years old and in college. I was given an assignment in one of my classes. The task was to write a paper about my life. I was charged with looking deep into certain aspects of my life's journey thus far. One of the areas I addressed in my report was my relationship with God and religion. Here is an excerpt of what I wrote back in 1972:

> *For me, religion and God is something very sacred and personal. I never really discuss God or my feelings about Him with anyone. It's just like we have a secret between ourselves, and we don't discuss it with anyone. I look toward Him for guidance, and He gives it to me in return. Who or what "He" is, I don't know. All I know is that He is there ...*

During that time in my life, I had not heard much about the term Spirituality. When looking into the definition of Spirituality and the role it plays in one's life, it became crystal clear to me that it is the driving force of life. "Spiritually" is commonly defined as "the quality of being concerned with the human spirit or soul as opposed to material or physical things." Often people use spirituality and religion interchangeably. They are treated the same when in reality, they are very different. This is not to say that one is better than the other. For many, they go hand and hand as we navigate throughout this life journey.

Religion is a set of practices and beliefs that are shared by a community or group of individuals. It usually does involve a relationship with GOD. I see "Religion" as more of an institutionalized system grounded in very strong beliefs, rituals, customs, and practices that govern our life. That is a good thing. In other words, as I have heard someone say, "Religion is how you live and not what you are called."

Spirituality, however, is more personal and is one person's relationships, as a human being. One may feel that Spirituality may or may not involve "GOD" but rather is our connection with our Spirit (GOD), Soul, and Body. Many call this power, this life force, many things such as God, Creator, Source, Higher Power, or Nature. It is internal and not external. In my early years of life, I may have struggled with all this. Today, I AM clear. We must each be aware of our own conscious connection with the Spiritual Source of Life.

In seeking my adult understanding of Spirituality, it became very clear to me that this does not refer to a church affiliation or religion. Spirituality looks at the ethics, morals, and relationship with, or belief in, a higher power and what you view as your purpose in life. I believe that each person has their own personal relationship with religion, spirituality, and God. There is no judgment. One has to do what works for them as an individual and to ensure that it is working for their best and highest good. In my personal coaching sessions with clients, I often ask them if what they are doing or involved in is effective, *"is this working for you?"* I know that–if they are honest–things are not working for them. With this newfound awareness, we can explore what will work for them–and so it is with you. It is important to be open to change and open to evolving throughout your life.

My first SPICE connection is Spirituality. It is the key that holds the purpose, wholeness of life, and balance we seek. It ensures all aspects or needs are fulfilled in the right way. When we adopt The Wheel of Life concept, only one aspect of life becomes the focus. The others are neglected. When this happens, we feel out of balance, and thus we are not happy, not content, and not at peace. Often we find ourselves walking around for years in this state. We feel out of control and out of sync with the world. When it becomes too much, we get to that Final Warning stage. It may come through you, or it may come from someone else to you. This is when you realize that you need to stop, take a moment, take a breath, and then take it all in. You'll see clearly, and you will know what to do. Remember my motto: *Awareness Builds Clarity* ™. Instead of Spirituality being a slice of your pie, you will see it as the circumference of your pie. Spirituality is the tie that binds your life experiences.

Putting in place the Spiritual Practices that are outlined in this book will assist you in gaining the balance needed. To know what is most important, what is most needed to survive, and the essentials for your life, you must first learn to surrender. This is not a bad or a defeated concept. You are not giving in or giving up; you are simply opening up to the goodness and the opportunities before you. It means that you surrender to the good and the greatness that is Divinely ordered for your life. Heed the warning and the call, listen and learn to be at peace. Spirituality is all about our consciousness. What are we telling ourselves each day, each hour, each second?

Do you know who you talk to the most throughout your life? Let me tell you! The person we talk to the most and the one we listen to the most—more than anyone else in this world—is not who you are probably thinking of right now. This person isn't your mother, your best friend, your minister, your counselor, your coworker. No. It most likely isn't GOD. Nope. The person you talk to the most is YOU! Yes, you. I know, right. Now, tell me I am wrong. I am pretty sure you won't because you know it is a true statement. You probably haven't thought of this before; but, now you know it is the honest truth. All we do all day long is self-talk. This self-talk determines our circumstances. What you may be going through at one time or another is direct feedback from what you are telling yourself. Direct from your own consciousness.

Always be sure that anything that comes from your mouth or that is in your mind is of higher consciousness. I have always known "whatever I think or whatever I say is my prayer" and affirmation. I ask myself often, "Is this something you want to manifest in your life?" If it is not the case, I immediately retract, cancel, or delete the thought from my thought process. I take back the words. I then replace it with what is for my best and my highest good. There are many stories about how our self-talk changes the trajectory of our circumstances.

My Spiritual connection tools and attributes have ushered me through many life events. Through consciously connecting to my Spirituality, I am still standing and thriving today. There were several times when I was convinced I would not make it through. Before I reached the age of 25, I'd experienced the transitions of a number of people in my life—my maternal and paternal grandmothers, my mother, and my sister. After 25, I experienced more transitions: my father, uncles, and aunties all transitioned early in my life. After these transitions, it continued with close friends, mentors, spiritual advisors— and just has never seemed to stop. Because of this, I struggled with the fear of loss. As I reflect on "failed" relationships, I recall way too many to name; however, I know that with each relationship, I learned more and more about myself and that they were not failures but rather necessities for my growth. I wouldn't change anything about that part of my journey. I soon learned that after each relationship, I bought something new for me as a form of self-care (but those are stories for another time). They all brought me closer to God. My professional world included its fair share of roadblocks, pitfalls, and potholes. Imagine having 45 years of documented exemplary work history and then getting fired. Imagine the mistreatment and micro-aggressions I tuned out along the way. Each situation, each scenario, each experience has a story. And each challenging story caused me heartache and pain. I stand as more than a survivor. I stand as a person who has moved from merely surviving to someone who is thriving and helping others along their respective paths. My desire is for you to first become a survivor, and then once you get grounded, thrive and flourish! Why? Because we all have Spiritual Practices that work.

THE S.P.I.C.E. OF LIFE

I'd like to share my Spiritual Heart Symbols. Each of these brings JOY, Comfort, and or Peace to my life. Whenever I receive them or see them, I beam with happiness. They bring me strength based on the story or meaning behind them. We all have these symbols in our lives. Often we may not even realize what they are or what they do for us. Here are mine:

Symbols	Inspired by...	Vibration or Power
Angel	My Ancestors	Faith, Love, Strength Intelligence; Purity, Comfort; Protection, Messengers
Bird-of-Paradise Flower	My parents, Luther and Delores Keyes	Paradise on Earth; faithfulness; the future beauty and freedom
Butterfly	Rev. Juanita Dunn; Bishop Dr. Barbara Lewis King	Transformation; growth and progress; spiritual rebirth; persistence and perseverance
Eagle	My dad, Luther Keyes; my brother, Kamau Daaood	Fly above all the negativity; go toward goals and dreams; trust the journey

THE S.P.I.C.E. OF LIFE

Symbols	Inspired by...	Vibration or Power
 **Hummingbird**	Aunt Linda Gage and Uncle Charles Gage	Happiness and joy; freedom; care-free; high vibrations; enjoy life and its simple pleasures
 **Rose**	My maternal grandmother, Edith; paternal grandmother, Ida	Inner strength; Beauty; The GOD Within

What are your Spiritual Heart Symbols? Sketch them below:

THE S.P.I.C.E. OF LIFE

Spirituality
Spiritual Practices from A to Z

Each of us has tried and true Spiritual Practices. A spiritual practice is any regular, intentional activity that helps us nourish and strengthen our personal relationship and connection with our Divine self. Spiritual practices bring balance to our lives. They give us strength, power, and purpose. They are what keeps us grounded and the reason we survive and thrive, despite what comes our way.

What follows is a list of 26 Spiritual Practices from A to Z that I use regularly. I use them when needed. I may use B, Q, and X one day. I may use A every morning. I may use D, E, I, O, U, and sometimes Y! I tailor how and when I use my Spiritual Practices.

Feel free to adapt and adopt practices from my list. More than anything, I encourage you to create and use your own list of Spiritual Practices. You are still standing, so they work! You are an individual; therefore, you must individualize the practices Divinely designed for you.

Adapt Daily Divine Nurturing Words: *"Today is the day the Lord has made, I will rejoice and be glad in it." Psalms 118:24*

Breathe Deeply; Exhale Completely: *Take a moment. Take a Breath. Take it all in. Before you do anything.*

Choose Knowing that with Your Power of Choice, You Create Your World: *Call on your Divine Imagination!*

Demonstrate the Practice of Letting Go: *Let go and let God. As my minister would say, quoting Ralph Waldo Emerson,*

THE S.P.I.C.E. OF LIFE

"Get your bloated nothingness out of the way of the divine circuits."

Evolve Into Living More of Your Spiritual-self Versus Your Human-self: *You are a Spiritual Being living a Human life.*

Forgive and be Forgiven: *Forgiveness is the most healing practice you can do for yourself.*

Gather Around Like-minded People: *Engage and share space with people from your neighborhood, church, faith community, or a positive group of individuals with similar values.*

Harness the Power of a Mantra: *A mantra can be a word or a sound that helps you to concentrate and meditate; it is something repeated in your mind or openly and outwardly.*

Inspire Others (and Yourself): *A kind word of encouragement, simple smile of approval, and expression of admiration can make someone's day. Indeed, when you inspire others, you inspire yourself.*

Job's Patience and Faith: *No matter what appears to be going wrong, no matter what feels uncomfortable, keep your faith, believe, and know your truth. No matter what!*

Keep Your Head to the Sky: *Always be a "Balcony" person pursuing the Upper Room with high vibrations and high energy.*

Learn to be in the Silence: *To be still and know is one of the most powerful things you can do. Peace be still.*

Meditate: *Embrace the quietness and listen for your inner voice.*

Never and No: *It is ok to say "no"; "No" and "never" can be freeing. They can be healing. Choose wisely when using them.*

Open Your Heart: *Always lead with your heart in everything you do.*

THE S.P.I.C.E. OF LIFE

Practice Purposeful Acts of Kindness: *Pay it forward to someone just because.*

Quiet Your Environment: *Retreat from stressful conditions, situations, and people; then, go into your cozy private peaceful internal world.*

Read Uplifting and Inspiring Writings: *Read to yourself—or to others—poetry, books, and scriptures, or other sacred texts.*

Sing Uplifting and Inspiring Songs: *Whether you sing or simply listen to music, open yourself to messages of joy, hope, healing, love, and inspiration.*

Turn Inward and Get Centered: *Devote time throughout the week for meditation, prayer, yoga, tai chi, tapping, energy work, and other practices that ground, center, and energize you.*

Unlock Understanding: *Devote time to seeking understanding and clarity about people, places, and things by being sympathetic, empathetic, and compassionate.*

Vision-casting leads us to the desires of our hearts: *Use vision casting and visualization techniques to bring focus to your life and realize your dreams and desires.*

Wash Feet to Open Spiritual Floodgates: *Devote time to periodically washing your feet or the feet of someone else. Foot-washing is a meaningful, spiritual experience that will teach you many things, including humility and service.*

X-ray and Analyze: *Use your Third Eye to see God and The Truth in all people, places, and things.*

Yes: *Say "YES" to the universe and universal laws of life. Much like "No," the word "Yes" is a full sentence. It, too, can be healing. Choose wisely when saying Yes!*

Zeal: *Maintain great energy and enthusiasm; stay in pursuit of a Divine and meaningful life.*

THE S.P.I.C.E. OF LIFE

It's your turn now! How might you adapt or adopt Spiritual Practices from my list? How might you create and use your own list of practices Divinely designed for you?

Spiritual Practice 1: _____

_____

Spiritual Practice 2: _____

_____

Spiritual Practice 3: _____

_____

Spiritual Practice 4: _____

_____

Spiritual Practice 5: _____

_____

Spiritual Practice 6: _____

_____

Spiritual Practice 7: _____

_____

THE S.P.I.C.E. OF LIFE

Spirituality: Lessons Learned

Write your thoughts about these:

Does Spirituality fit in my life? If it does, where and how does it fit? If it doesn't, share your thoughts.

_____

_____

_____

_____

What is one Spiritual Practice that I will START now that will benefit my life's journey?

_____

_____

_____

What is one Spiritual Practice that I will KEEP using because it has consistently worked for me?

_____

_____

_____

What is one Spiritual Practice that I must STOP because it is not for my best and highest good?

_____

_____

THE S.P.I.C.E. OF LIFE

As I reflect on Spirituality, what do I believe?

As I reflect on Spirituality, what do I know is:

What is my affirmation for my Spiritually? What is my overall goal?

What are some Divine Nurturing Words of comfort and peace for Spiritually?

THE S.P.I.C.E. OF LIFE

My Spirituality Story

Reflect on your life and think about your Spirituality Story. Did your childhood—or an experience—form or shape you as a spiritual being? If either did, how so? Use this space to write your Spiritual Story. You may consider your thoughts from "Spirituality: Lessons Learned" to help you write your story.

THE S.P.I.C.E. OF LIFE

THE S.P.I.C.E. OF LIFE

THE S.P.I.C.E. OF LIFE

NOTES ON SPIRITUALITY

Personal Growth and Development

PERSONAL GROWTH
AND DEVELOPMENT

Personal Growth and Development bring to focus the trinity of MIND, BODY, and SOUL, which encompasses our overall health. I am sure you are like me. We all strive to reach a perfect level of health and wellbeing. This includes our physical fitness, nutrition, stress levels, mental health, and overall healthiness for your lifestyle. This also includes our education and career paths that guide us to and through a meaningful life.

Personal Health

Let me tell you my personal story: I was brought up in a household where— although we were not perfect—we were raised in a pure loving environment. We had our challenges as families do, and I truly believe my parents made sure they taught us how to be healthy, eat healthily, stay physically active, and be mentally strong individuals. Even though they had their shortcomings, I knew they wanted to teach us the right way. Sometimes by telling us, other times through their examples. My parents and grandparents were my role models. I studied what they did or what they did not do in their daily lives. In my attempt to learn from them, I also did not want to make the same obvious mistakes they made during their lifetimes. I focused on not eating too much sugar or high fat, not smoking, or doing drugs. I made sure I stayed active. I was even a vegetarian for a very short period of time.

My older brother was my role model for living a healthy lifestyle. I learned a lot from him at that time and strived to be steadfast in eating a healthy diet. Other family members who did not really subscribe to this made it difficult for me to maintain this lifestyle. They would laugh and make fun of me. They told me I did not know what I was doing. They said that what I was doing could be harmful to my health if I was not making sure my body got all the nutrients it needed. I eventually decided to go to college to earn a degree in Health and Nutrition.

My mission and passion in life have been to help prevent diseases and sicknesses and promote health and wellness. Why? I believe it was because I witnessed so much illness and many deaths in my life. My mother was a smoker; she passed away at age 42 from lung cancer. My maternal grandmother passed away from colon cancer at the age of 52. My sister was killed by a drunk driver at age 18. My daddy died from congestive heart failure, complications from bone cancer. I could go on and on. Most—if not all —of these cases were lifestyle issues. They were preventable.

My goal in life was to avoid demise from unhealthy lifestyle choices by living a clean and healthy lifestyle. Yet through all of my efforts and the pain of losing my loved ones, I was still affected. I experienced adverse health and body conditions, mental health issues, and the overall health of my soul. Despite what I "thought" I was doing right, I developed life-threatening health issues anyway. My focus shifted from health prevention to health management. Yes, I had to take a really hard look at my life. I had to examine my lifestyle and make an investment in my livelihood. I had to secure the necessary knowledge and skills to live a healthful life.

The state of one's mental health is important. Poor mental health comes in many forms and stages. It is a common occurrence these days, even though most will not admit it. I knew that my mental health was compromised. And it was especially initially affected by the death of my mother when I was 20. She was so young. I was in that transition period where you become closer to your parents; you begin to have adult conversations. Maybe even becoming friends. I needed her in my life. My mother was beautiful, so sweet, so kind, so nurturing. She was funny, fun, and loving. At that time, I was engaged and pregnant with my son. During the nine months of my pregnancy, of this new life, mama was deteriorating and coming to the end of her life. She made her transition the day after her first grandson was born. The trauma of my mother's death was further compounded by my fiancé's decision to relocate out of state for college and not get married to me. He left me when I was eight months pregnant with our child. Mama was there for me as best she could be.

On the day my child was born, mama was in the hospital in a coma. I was told when my mother was informed that I had given birth, she must have heard them and understood because she released a sigh and made her transition within the next 10 hours. Everyone told me she was just waiting for her grandchild to be born. The transition of my mother and the loss of the love of my life hit pretty darn hard. Life felt heavy then. Although I carry some of that heaviness with me today, thankfully, it does not weigh me down. These traumatic experiences have fueled my healing work in transformation. In fact, this book is evidence of this work.

I tell this story not to evoke sadness. I share it to demonstrate you will survive the unthinkable. I am sure many of you reading this have had similar or worse experiences in your life. Many cannot cope. Many do not make it through those challenging periods. The truth is trauma can follow you throughout your life. Once you understand that it is not *what* happens to you but rather *how* you react to what happens to you that makes the difference, this becomes a critical tool. Once you learn these survival tools, you realize that life is a blessing, and you are already alright!

How have I survived? I have survived and thrived because I did not stop. My baby sister was killed by a drunk driver; I didn't stop. When daddy developed a rare form of cancer that took his life, I didn't stop. He never smoked or drank; he didn't "run the streets" but was an awesome provider. He was an honorable man in my eyes. Not perfect, but who really is? All of them were gone too soon.

For me, the deaths kept rolling in starting in the 1970s through today. I experienced death and loss at a very young age. Death is not often experienced by those so young. Death took its toll on me. If I were to diagnose myself, I would say I was functional yet depressed. I carried pain, hurt, and agony within. People simply did not know; most would never know. Keeping things bottled up can be very dangerous, though. This is one of the reasons many people don't make it. We suffer because we hold it all in. We won't talk to anyone or seek help. I believe I survived because I was blessed to have tremendous help and support from family, friends, and mentors. I have been helped by people who I did not know. I have dedicated my life to being a servant. Helping others was something that made me feel good. Sure, it was good, and I felt good; but, was it really good? It was all good until I lost myself in the process of helping everyone else. And in the end, I really wasn't helping anyone. I was enabling them and ignoring myself in the process. So instead of it being a win-win, it was more like a lose-lose. Rather than just sitting with this information, paralyzed, I began to listen for essential truths. I began to utilize my self-help practices. By using the practices and tips found in this book, I have grown and conquered this issue and many others. I have done so by taking notice of things that helped, lifted, and centered me. I began to invest in "Me." That is where it started. Yes, thank God I am still standing!

A Winning Investment: "YOU"

I have finally realized I must focus on being and staying healthy in my mind, body, and soul. We need to "know thyself." Our bodies are marvelously made, and if we study what makes us tick, we can live a long healthy life. I invite you to review my ABCs of investing in yourself. I offer 26 simple things we should KNOW about our bodies and DO for our wellbeing—things we should be aware of. If you focus on and stay tuned to each area, you will make a

THE S.P.I.C.E. OF LIFE

winning investment in YOU.

A. A1C measures the average amount of glucose (sugar) in your blood during the past 2-3 months. Maintaining a normal Hemoglobin A1C value will help reduce the risk of long-term problems from diabetes.

B. Blood Pressure is the pressure of circulating blood on the walls of blood vessels. The heart is working to pump blood through the circulatory system. If this is not normal, it can lead to hypertension and its complications. This is often called a silent killer.

C. Cholesterol is associated with coronary heart disease. Maintaining a normal cholesterol value will promote heart health, among other things.

D. Diet includes the types of food we habitually consume. We all have a diet. We must be aware of how we use diet to lose weight, for medical reasons, or to maintain a healthy lifestyle. Regardless of how we use our diet, it is important to make sure we give our bodies the nutrients, vitamins, and minerals needed to sustain life.

E. Exercise takes many forms, and the key is this: you must keep moving to keep moving throughout your life.

F. Fresh Air, regardless of the time of year, will improve physical and mental health. You should always get fresh outdoor air; the more, the better. Get some Vitamin D.

G. Gratitude is important, so begin and end each day with thankfulness.

THE S.P.I.C.E. OF LIFE

H. Humor is great medicine and is good for Heart Health and Mental health. It reduces stress, and it just feels so good to laugh.

I. Intentions have the power to shape your reality. Be intentional and specific about the desires of your heart. Keep your attention on your intentions.

J. Journaling helps tremendously with clearing your mind, relieving stress, and creating space for ongoing self-reflecting. Keeping a journal helps you organize your mind and evokes mindfulness. Writing is therapeutic; get it out!

K. Kindness returns to us blessed and multiplied, so practice kindness every day with everyone you encounter.

L. Limits are like good fences; they establish boundaries and offer protections. It is important to know your personal and mental limits. Exercise them and let them be known.

M. Medical Check-ups are essential to living a life of health and wellness. "Know thyself." Be in tune and on top of what is happening in your body.

N. Nutrition is about providing the food necessary for optimal health and growth. Good nutrition goes hand in hand with fitness. In fact, you cannot out "train" or out "workout" poor nutrition.

O. Oral Health gives clues about your overall health. There is a mouth-body connection. Poor oral health can create other health issues.

P. Passion drives us. Do you know and live your life's passion? It is your motivation. It is your "WHY."

THE S.P.I.C.E. OF LIFE

Passion is that strong urge or emotion that guides you and propels you to your ultimate successes in life.

Q. Quiet Time is essential to your ongoing renewal. Devote time to daily prayer and meditation. It can also simply be a time sitting in silence. "Peace be still" … so powerful!

R. Rest, relaxation, and sleep are essential for our overall health and wellbeing. Relaxation could be found while sitting on a porch with a glass of wine. It could be alone time with you and Sudoku. It could be a midday nap. Peaceful rest increases productivity and mental clarity. Take the time to get proper and enough sleep daily. A Must!

S. **Stress** can be positive or negative, good or bad. Remember this. Take a moment to notice and understand your stress triggers. Work to minimize or eliminate triggers of bad stress and learn how to benefit from the triggers of good stress.

T. Tests, when taken according to our age and lifestyle, can help us screen for various health challenges. Prevention is the goal, so be open to screening tests taken at regular intervals.

U. Usefulness is a feeling many of us desire. We want to know that we are useful to ourselves and others. In fact, I find that the more I can do for others (whether service, gifts, or loving-kindness), the better I feel.

V. Vision has less to do with the eyes and more to do with the mind. It is our ability to envision within ourselves what we desire to achieve in any area of our lives.

W. Water makes up between 50% and 70% of the human body weight. Hydration is critical for every part of our body. Water and proper hydration are beneficial as they flush the body, regulate body temperature, help with brain function, and have a calming and purifying effect.

X. **EXtraordinary** is who and what we are, so be remarkable, be unusually great. Allow yourself to radiate and beam!

Y. Yoga is great for physical and mental well-being. It has many health benefits. You may also consider health modalities such as Tai Chi.

Z. Zeal and zest for living convey your high energy of excitement and enthusiasm. Those vibrations yield health and wellness.

Personal Development

Education and Career are integral to your personal development. In this process or slice of your pie, you are learning new things. More importantly, education is an enlightening experience that we start from the time we are born, maybe even when we're in the womb. It is important to understand that life is our teacher. People, places, things, and all experiences are teaching us every day, every moment. Education is an ongoing process, whether it be systematic, structured, and academic, or if it is organically gained from simply living life. Most people think learning ends with school or college. The truth is learning begins at birth and continues with until your last breath. By osmosis, we gradually and often unconsciously gain knowledge, ideas, and skills. The University of Life is always in session, and we must pay attention. It has a key purpose in our life.

Education is always a section of *The SPICE of Life Wheel* ^TM, and we are often asked if we are satisfied with the time we devote to learning and education. The answer is always "Yes" when we see education as a lifelong process. It's a "Yes" when we take a serious look into how we are educated every day. Education comes to us in many ways: formal, non-formal, informal, distance, remote, virtual, and life lessons. In fact, I believe life lessons are the most valuable education one will ever receive.

Education—specifically, our life lessons—notes philosophers, is not the name of a particular activity. Education encompasses different activities, experiences, and processes that mainly bring into focus the social aspects of human beings. Education is not static. Education is a continuous and lifelong process. I have always valued education highly because I believe it helps people develop their capacities, thereby empowering them to fulfill their possibilities. The physical and mental maturity of a person also depends upon one's interactions and adjustments to the situation and circumstances in our lives.

Our education offers us gradual growth and development. Certain individuals, groups, and institutions contribute significantly. Knowledge about self, the immediate physical and social environment, and the world experiences play huge parts in our evolution throughout life. As we know, our very first learning takes place in our family environment. Our habits, attitude, skills, and interests are formulated during this time. We learn new things by listening, observing, and doing simple, informal things that shape us as human beings. Living among family members during our informative years and launching into an environment where we interact with others besides our family adds growth and new experiences. This learning deliberately does not take place in a formal situation, and it is generally called informal education. This natural learning is usually the result of the social and physical surroundings in which we live. Much of our education takes place subconsciously. We don't know what we don't know; as life unfolds, answers become clear. For sure, Awareness Builds Clarity! We become aware through this process of life.

When "education" is deliberately planned, it is called formal education. It encompasses the existing structured primary and secondary school system. It also includes the college and university systems. Our formal education can lead us to choose a lifetime career. Sometimes, however, experiences in life other than a formal education can lead us to our chosen profession. Family business, internships, volunteer service, and job-shadowing allow us to see others pursue work in fields that may grow into interests for us. These interests can easily form our lifetime career paths. When we extend the educational phase—whether formally or informally—into a career, we focus our attention on three important areas:

Life Planning includes all areas where you plan in your life: goal setting, plans for family, financial and estate planning, planning for your lifestyle, life transition planning, and how well you manage your time and your energy. Some people plan day-by-day, others week-by-week or month-to-month. The most successful people plan for the long term, such as 5, 10, or more years in advance. This takes skill and a focused effort. What areas of your life require planning?

Work or employment includes your job, ways you earn money, your career path to earn a sustainable income, and strategies to reach your career goals in life. What are your ambitions to manage and lead others or establish your own business?

Finances include goal setting, managing your finances, network, streams of income, and your money consciousness. Whatever you think about and focus on, you will surely bring about. Always think big. Norman Vincent Peale often noted, "shoot for the moon, and even if you miss, you'll land amongst the stars." You will be closer to your target as you keep focused and pushing. What is your money consciousness? Do you have a middle-class or a millionaire mindset?

All of this takes time, commitment, and perseverance. It takes a "stick-to-it" consciousness and a "quitting is not an option" mentality.

Let me tell you a quick story about a young student. This includes her life lessons, formal education, and pursuit of happiness. She came from a good family. Parents were supportive. Both parents worked. Only one parent had attended college. She was determined to make something of her life. She went to college and graduated with a Bachelor's degree. She aspired to become a Registered Dietitian (RD). She always wanted to help people in some way and first wanted to be a social worker. Her father was not feeling a social worker, so he suggested that she take another route and go into the health field. An RD was health-related, and "How hard could that be?," she thought. There were several pathways for her to take to reach this goal. She was a single mom and struggled to go to college in the first place while raising a child. She became a mom at age 20. She had plans for marriage, but the father had different plans and left her.

She worked hard to complete her bachelor's degree. In order to become a Registered Dietitian, however, she had to either get into an internship program or receive her Master's Degree. Due to her circumstances, she could not get into the internship program. This young woman had to work full-time in order to take care of her young toddler son. She took the master's degree path because she could work this around her work schedule. This was very difficult at the time, but she had to enter the Master's program in order to become an RD. She struggled and second-guessed herself, trying to accomplish this, but without it, she really could neither obtain the career she desired nor could she make the salary she deserved in the field. This young mom worked hard to learn about all aspects of the field without the hands-on experience she could have received if she had gone through an internship program.

This young person had to complete her master's degree. Although it was challenging, she managed to complete all the classes within the required time frame, and then she had to take a Composition Examination in order to graduate with her Master's degree. Unfortunately, she did not receive a passing grade; she flopped on one of the required areas on the exam. Therefore, she had to take the entire exam again. She could not just take the question she did not pass; she actually had to retake the entire Composition Examination over again. As the determined soul that she was, she studied hard again and re-took the exam. It was very difficult for her but she eventually passed and received her Master's Degree. This put her closer to her overall goal of being an RD. But to become a Registered Dietitian, she had to also successfully pass a national credentialing exam.

With her Master's, she was now eligible to take the Registration Exam. This was a very comprehensive exam, similar to passing the Bar Exam for lawyers. She studied with a study group and studied on her own, but she did not have the hands-on experience she would have had if she had the luxury of participating in an internship program.

The RD exam was taken. Nowadays, we have the technology to receive the results in real-time. Back in those days, students had to wait for a letter to be mailed, and it took a couple of weeks to reach you. When the letter arrived, she anxiously opened it, and the first line was "We regret to inform you" … she did not pass. You had to have a score of over 75 points. She had the opportunity to take the exam again. She studied the areas where she fell short and took it for the second time.

When the second letter arrived, she opened it, and it read, "We regret ..." She did not pass again, only by 5 points, but still failed. Yes, she cried. She wanted to give up, but she knew she could do this. She studied hard again and re-took the exam several months later. You would think the third time was a charm. When the result letter arrived, she said a prayer, knowing this time for sure she would have a successful outcome. Hesitantly, she opened it, and once again, it stated, "We regret ..." was on the first line. At that point, she was done. The negative self-talk took over; "I cannot do this," "who do I think I am, trying to be something that I am not." She felt that she should just get a regular job or get welfare assistance. As a single mom, she was working full time and attending school full time. She just felt defeated. She knew, however, she had come too far to stop now. She took a deep breath, said a little prayer, seeking God for guidance. Her answer was, "take it again." And she did. When the fourth result letter arrived, she was terrified to open it. What if ... , she thought. She opened it, and the first word was "Congratulations ..." "Oh my God," she cried, "I did it!" She had passed, barely, but a pass was a pass. She made it by two points; but heck, she made it! That was very hard, extremely challenging, and piercingly stressful, but it was her life, and with conviction and persistence, she made it.

This young woman continued to climb the professional ladder. She has been going, going ever since. This young woman went to work in her chosen profession. She advanced in the field, consistently moved up the ladder and chain of command. She became a Supervisor, a Manager, Local Director and then took a position as the Statewide Director! Today she is an Entrepreneur, Trainer, and Inspirational Speaker. Living her Best Life. Today she is the published author of this book. Yep, that's right. She is Me. Never give up on yourself!

This story is the cornerstone of this book. I really want to bring home the notion that if you have a goal, a dream, stay the course. Be persistent and believe in yourself. Even if it is not looking good, always remember *Quitting is not an Option*, and it will all pay off in the end.

Or is Quitting an Option. This came to me one day after I gave this talk, and a woman came up to me and said, "Thank you so much for your talk, I have been trying to make a decision about retiring. It has been a big decision for me. Now, after listening to you, I have made up my mind. I don't want to be a quitter. I am going to stay." I immediately said to her, "No, wait, wait, wait." It was important to make the distinction between quitting and making an informed decision to transition, to shift, to change in direction. It is imperative to know when it is time to move on. That can be a good thing. God may have something better for you than you could imagine for yourself.

I do not want anyone to feel that deciding to retire would be considered or looked upon as quitting because, clearly, if you are ready today and you've worked hard at your job for over 30-40 years, it is time for you to do YOU! Or even at a young age, if you are not feeling or getting the message that this is where I should be, you should move on to where the force is leading you. However, do not ever quit because it has become hard, or you cannot see yourself achieving your dreams or reaching your potential. That is always something you can overcome. If you have paid your dues, so to speak, or if it is time to move on or shift to something that is for your highest and best good, by all means, do it. I said to her, "Child, retire and invite me to your retirement party." This represents not quitting but rather shifting. And that is a good thing.

"It is your Choice"
Patience, Perseverance, and Persistence are Power

"When you find yourself on the edge, when the clouds of darkness knock you off your guard, just remember who you are" (a Phyllis Hyman song lyric). One important fact to always remember is that you have POWER, and you can use your Power to make Choices that reflect your best and highest good. It has been said many times, "Only we can give away our power." You must keep it. The use of daily Affirmations is powerful. An affirmation is your tool to solidify, encourage and provide self-emotional support.

Here are a few affirmations that I have created to remind me of my POWER to make my own Choices in my life's direction. These have sustained me and lifted me higher and higher, no matter what has come my way. We must always have words, affirmations, prayers, songs, and whatever resonates with you, that are perfect for any situation and circumstances that are not in line with your good and your life's purpose.

I have listed Circumstances and Affirmations from A to Z. These entries are areas I believe we have the Power to Choose to be or live our lives in such a manner that will sustain us and set us free from any condition or situation we are going and growing through. I know this because they work for me. Remember, "I still stand." What has worked for you? You are still standing; you are still here. Choose to use these affirmations daily as needed, or better yet, create/write your own in the following spaces.

AFFIRMATIONS from A to Z:

A – AWAKEN – Has a physical and metaphysical connotation. Waking up from sleeping. Something we must do every day in order to move forth with our daily goals. More importantly, once we are awake, we must become completely conscious, mentally perceptive, and responsive to what lies ahead of us each day. To realize your dreams and goals you must first wake up!

"Today I CHOOSE to use my POWER to AWAKE physically from sleep each morning to a consciousness of being perfect, whole and complete."

_____

_____

_____

_____

THE S.P.I.C.E. OF LIFE

B – BREATHE – This is a must each day of our lives and throughout our days. Sounds silly to say because, of course, we are breathing, right? But are we? We must take mindful and conscious Breaths. Always take a moment, take a breath and take it all in. It centers one's spirit and gives you clarity and a sense of peace, no matter what you are currently facing. We are taking air in and expelling air from our lungs. This is the power of breathing life. One can neither breathe for yesterday nor for tomorrow. Therefore, when we breathe we are in the current moment. We are experiencing the Presence.

"Today I CHOOSE to use my POWER to BREATHE in the Love, the Light, and the Essence of Life, and to exhale any and all things that are not for my best and highest good."

C – CONNECT with thankfulness and gratitude to your source, with your higher power, with the Most High. Keep a conscious connection with life and all that surrounds you.

"Today I CHOOSE to use my POWER and Exercise my Conscious Connection with the food I eat, the air I breathe, and the water I drink; that is my Perfect Life Source."

_____

_____

_____

D – DARE TO BE YOU! Have the courage. Challenge yourself to be brave. Do not let anyone determine who you are. Speak up for yourself.

"Today, I CHOOSE to use my POWER to shine my Light on any situation that appears to be in the dark."

_____

_____

_____

E – ENERGIZE yourself. You must keep moving to keep Moving. This starts the circulation that energizes you daily.

"Today, I CHOOSE to use my POWER and energize myself to take thoughtful action that builds me up and renews my strength and yields vitality."

_____

_____

_____

F – FORGIVE – Forgiveness is one of the most powerful, healing things one can do that will eliminate any fear, barriers and blockages standing in your way of living a fulfilled and purposeful life.

"Today, I CHOOSE to use my POWER and forgive myself and others for any wrongs I have felt was done to me or that I may have done to others. I shower myself and others with unconditional Love, now and forever."

G – GET UP – Get out of bed. Now that you have the positive thoughts in your head, say a prayer or affirmation. Put your daily plan into action and put the days' purpose on display.

"Today, I CHOOSE to use my POWER to get up, get out and show out!"

H – HONOR – Always give yourself the utmost respect and hold yourself in the highest esteem.

"Today, I CHOOSE to use my POWER to Honor myself and others. I am honorable, and I will keep my agreements and treat others with respect."

THE S.P.I.C.E. OF LIFE

I – INSPIRE – Always know that regardless of what is going on in your life, you can still inspire others. Your stories are testimonies and encourage others to continue.

"Today, I CHOOSE to use my POWER to inspire positive creations that have long- lasting consequences for the universe."

J – JUMP UP – Show your enthusiasm, jump to the opportunity. If you are too slow you will miss out …

"Today, I CHOOSE to use my POWER to jump high and fast, to open the door to opportunities that lie ahead for me."

K – KEEP UP – During these times, there are so many modes to stay in the information loop. We are in the social media age, and it is vitally important to stay on top of these avenues. Make sure that you are reading, studying, and networking to stay informed. Knowledge is powerful, as we know.

"Today, I CHOOSE to use my POWER to keep up, with all that is going on around me, to stay current and ready for anything that comes my way."

L – LIVE, LAUGH, LOVE – We only have this one life (as far as I know). So make it the best life it can be. Do what makes you laugh, what brings you joy, and what fills your heart with love.

"Today, I CHOOSE to use my POWER to show my Love with thoughtful acts, kind words, and affection."

M – MEDITATE – One of the most powerful, healing, and harmonizing things one can do. Communication with God, Spirit, the universe, and nature. Meditation is the act of becoming still and listening to the messages from within that bring you to a state of calm and peace. Practice Meditation at least once a day. The more, the merrier.

"Today, I CHOOSE to use my POWER to meditate daily and listen to the still small voice within."

N – NETWORK – Connecting with like-minded individuals, those with the same affinity, heading in or already in the same direction in life as you are going.

"Today, I CHOOSE to use my POWER to and connect with like-minded individuals so that we can share ideas and support one another to the top."

O – OPEN your heart and tap into your creativity. Open up and step out there. Embrace change; it is a constant in life. Be open and receptive to become the greater you.

"Today, I CHOOSE to use my POWER and put my creativity up front and center for all to see, hear, and enjoy!"

THE S.P.I.C.E. OF LIFE

_____

_____

_____

P – POLISH – You always shine, and at times we dull ourselves by our actions and words and thoughts. Work daily to shine your inner Light.

"Today, I CHOOSE to use my POWER to illuminate my Bright Light in all aspects of my life!"

_____

_____

_____

Q – QUIT taking it personally!

"Today, I CHOOSE to use my POWER to know that what you think about me is none of my business."

_____

_____

_____

R – REST – You must take the time to STOP, lie down, slow down, rest, and remove anything that is not in your best interest. Eliminate obstacles, negativity, and habits as well as negative people. Tap into the power of sleep.

THE S.P.I.C.E. OF LIFE

"Today, I CHOOSE to use my POWER to take conscious time to turn within and allow my Mind, Body, and Soul to rest and rejuvenate."

_____

_____

_____

_____

S – SPEAK – Your words matter. Be kind to others as well as yourself. Communicate with full confidence your desires, concerns, dreams, beliefs, and ideas will manifest. Step out of your comfort zone.

"Today, I CHOOSE to use my POWER to deliberately speak to and protect my mental, emotional, and spiritual state of mind. To always speak kindly to myself and others."

_____

_____

_____

_____

T – THRIVE – Move beyond just making it or mere survival. You have within you the ability to thrive and flourish.

"Today, I CHOOSE to use my POWER to move beyond my wildest dreams and desires and to Know it is already done in the mind of GOD."

U – UNDERSTAND – Seek to understand. Do not go around saying, "I am confused." This will keep you in a state of confusion. You seek to understand, to be in the know. Instead, say, "please help me to better understand, to be clear."

"Today, I CHOOSE to use my POWER to seek to understand and live in a state of clarity on any situation or circumstances I am facing."

V – VISION – Take time to sit and become quiet. Vision comes from a higher power. This is actually listening to the still small voice within.

"Today, I CHOOSE to use my POWER to be open and receptive to the voice, sights, and sounds from within and to follow and trust the Vision given to me knowing it is for my perfect and Highest Good."

W – WORSHIP is an act of giving time for devotion and recognition of God.

"Today, I CHOOSE to use my POWER to praise God, the higher power in my life, and to know that God is always with me, never to leave me."

X – EXHALE – Seek to breathe out in a deliberate manner, rid yourself of any and everything that is not for your best and highest Good. Exhale in order to open your Sacred Space for Love, Peace, Harmony, and Joy.

"Today, I CHOOSE to use my POWER to Exhale all that is not like me and to inhale and demonstrate the healing powers of Love, Peace, fHarmony, and Joy."

Y – YELL—INTERNALLY or EXTERNALLY—aloud delight. Sometimes you just have to let it out! To release the

Joy for the world to hear and to see. This is an exhilarating feeling.

> *"Today, I CHOOSE to use my POWER to YELL*
> *at the top of my Lungs. I am proactive,*
> *patient, persistent, and powerful!"*

Z – ZEAL – The powerful feeling to go forward and be! To express an urge to go on.

> *"Today, I CHOOSE to use my POWER to go forth and*
> *not look back, to live in the Divine Present."*

THE S.P.I.C.E. OF LIFE

PERSONAL LIFE INVESTMENT PLAN INTRODUCTION

I learned early in life that I needed to develop a Personal Life Investment Plan. This is something we often do for our jobs/work or our finances, but we rarely ever take the time to invest in ourselves. We do not put a plan of action in place for areas in our personal life. As Warren Buffet said, "The best investment you can make is an investment in yourself."

I am a believer that one must take time to focus on how our day-to-day choices, decisions, actions, thoughts, words, and experiences are affecting our life. All of these entities are responsible for where you are today and where you'll be tomorrow. Whether you want to believe it or not, taking a close look at how such things as our Faith, Beliefs, and Truths are a reflection of our current situations in our relationships, careers, finances, health, and overall well-being. This will provide you with information that will change your life for the better. Dive deep into your current state of Personal being-ness and set in motion your Personal and Spiritual journey. We all have fears, barriers and blockages that get in the way of us living our best and authentic lives. There are memorable ways to conquer fears, barriers, and blocks that "appear" to interfere with our intentions, our growth, and our goals in life. One must be ready to face their Truth, and take the Divine Journey into knowing Thyself.

The following exercise will set you on a trajectory that is for your best and highest good. Take the time to sit and be still, look at your life and where you feel you are not successful, and make a plan that will move you forward in aligning your life with positive outcomes. Often when individuals do this, they find a lot of areas in need. Pick just one goal to start with that is easy and short-term. Once you understand the process, you can begin to tackle the more involved and long-term goals.

For example, an easy short-term plan can be to lose weight. A more involved long-term plan can be to get your Master's Degree or to start your own business. Focus on a goal that you are committed to complete.

It's your turn now! I'd like you to use the next few pages to help you develop your own Personal Life Investment Plan. Take your time. Put serious thoughts into your answers and your plan.

PERSONAL LIFE INVESTMENT PLAN

VISION: Your vision is a clear mental picture of what you want to achieve for your life. If you do not know what you want to do with your life, begin by calling your Divine Life Plan into expression through Visioning. Write down God's vision for you. Vision is about the possibilities that you see, the potential for you to improve professionally and personally. Your vision is what you see for yourself. In developing your vision, it is suggested that you learn to meditate, to be still, and invoke God's/The Universe's plan for your life. *What is Your Vision?*

_____

_____

_____

THE S.P.I.C.E. OF LIFE

_____

_____

_____

_____

PURPOSE: Your "WHY." First, you should be an observer of your life. This can only be done with accurate observations of your actions and your feelings. When one truly lives one's purpose, it creates the ultimate sense of Peace, Love, and Euphoria. Second, you strive to live your purpose; lead a purposeful, purpose-filled life. **What is Your Purpose?**

_____

_____

_____

_____

_____

_____

MISSION: Your life's mission is what you are here to do. The mission includes the specific actions, tasks, and goals that it takes to realize the vision and purpose of your "why." Consider your mission to be very important because it will be the heart of your entire existence. Your mission needs to be personalized. Determine what Drives You, your Passion, what you can do/be the Best at. Your true mission may be your total life plan/existence **or** specifics such as your health, happiness, abundance, spiritual practices, relationships, elevating your consciousness, or whatever you desire. Write down your personal Mission Statement. *What is Your Mission Statement?*

VALUE: What is worth investing in and keeping—your principles or standards of behavior that are most important to you in life. One should have at least five core values you live by. *What are your top 5 Values (feel free to write more than 5)?*

THE S.P.I.C.E. OF LIFE

GOALS: Affirming what you will accomplish in your Divine Life Plan. Use your own words with conviction and certainty. List your Goal(s):

- *Short-Term Goals* – You determine, Monthly, Quarterly, or Yearly is recommended
- *Intermediate Goals* – 2 to 4 Years
- *Long-Term Goals* – These are goals that are usually 5 to 10 years
- Each intermediate and short-term goal should be made with long-term strategies in mind.
- Goal setting is one of the areas that you will likely need assistance with, so there is no better way to practice this than learning to set your own goals.

What Are Your <u>Goals</u>?
Short

_____

_____

_____

_____

_____

_____

Intermediate

_____

_____

Long or Life Time

OBJECTIVES: Set in motion what, when, where, how, and maybe even why you are on this journey or path. Your Objectives should be Specific, Measurable, Attainable, Achievable, Relevant, Realistic or Tangible, and Time-Sensitive. You will have at least one Objective for each Goal, no more than three.

What are Your <u>Objectives</u> for each Goal listed:
Goal One

_____

_____

_____

Goal Two

_____

_____

_____

_____

_____

_____

Goal Three

_____

_____

_____

_____

_____

_____

STEPS: Begin to put your Divinely Ordered Vision into actions. Make them realistic and doable, and make sure they are in line with your Purpose, Mission, Goals, and Objectives.

What are Your <u>Steps</u> for each Objective?

THE S.P.I.C.E. OF LIFE

Goal One: *Objective #1, #2, #3*

_____

_____

_____

_____

_____

_____

_____

Goal Two: *Objective #1, #2, #3*

_____

_____

_____

_____

_____

_____

Goal Three: *Objective #1, #2, #3*

_____

_____

_____

_____

_____

_____

THE S.P.I.C.E. OF LIFE

SUSTAINABILITY: How will you ensure you maintain your Action plan? The use of Daily Practices, such as watching your words and thoughts, using poems, affirmations, uplifting songs, bible verses, mantras, symbols, prayer, meditation, and visioning. These will help you to sustain your progress and stay on point.

What is Your Sustainability Plan of action?

THE S.P.I.C.E. OF LIFE

Personal Growth and Development Lessons Learned

Write your thoughts about these:

Does Personal Growth and Development fit in my life? If it does, where and how does it fit? If it doesn't, share your thoughts. How healthy are my mind, body, and soul?

_____

_____

_____

What is one Personal Growth and Development Practice that I will START now that will benefit my life's journey?

_____

_____

_____

_____

What is one Personal Growth and Development Practice that I will KEEP using because it has consistently worked for me?

_____

_____

_____

_____

THE S.P.I.C.E. OF LIFE

What is one Personal Growth and Development Practice that I must STOP because it is not for my best and highest good?

_____

_____

_____

As I reflect on Personal Growth and Development, what do I believe?

_____

_____

_____

As I reflect on Personal Growth and Development, what do I know?

_____

_____

_____

What is my affirmation for my Personal Growth and Development? What is my overall goal?

_____

_____

_____

_____

THE S.P.I.C.E. OF LIFE

What are some Divine Nurturing Words of comfort and peace for Personal Growth and Development?

THE S.P.I.C.E. OF LIFE

My Personal Growth and Development Story

Reflect on your life and think about your Personal Growth and Development Story. Did your childhood– or an experience–form or shape your personal growth and development? If either did, how so? Use this space to write your Personal Growth and Development Story. You may consider your thoughts from "Personal Growth and Development: Lessons Learned" to help you with writing your story.

THE S.P.I.C.E. OF LIFE

THE S.P.I.C.E. OF LIFE

NOTES ON PERSONAL GROWTH AND DEVELOPMENT

Introspection

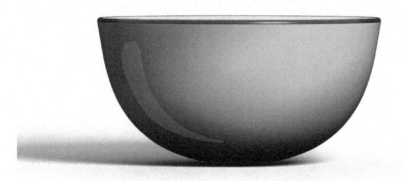

INTROSPECTION

I often wondered, who AM I? Why do I function and act the way I do? I have always felt I am so different from most people. I think differently than others. It has been this way all my life. I have often felt out of place in certain settings. Although I was teased and maligned by some family and friends, I always felt comfortable enough with myself to be there. I just took it in, sucked it up, and kept moving. One of my traits felt simultaneously "good" and "not so good" in my spirit. I realized I have a need or desire to please people. Yeah, I guess I am one of those "people pleasers." I want people to be happy; at times, this happiness is at the expense of my own happiness. This is why you might hear me say, "whatever you want, I don't care." I have always had the "fix it" syndrome. If there was any discourse or issues among my family members, my friends, or co-workers, I would, for whatever reason, think I had to fix the issue or situation. When I was successful, I felt better and at peace. My friends or family members can tell you stories where "Debbie forced us to get together and work it out," or, for example, when a member of my family would steal my daddy's car keys to go joyriding, I would hide the keys so they couldn't find them. Then no one would get caught, which would yield peace of mind for me. That one kinda backfired because I would forget to put the keys back, and daddy would be frantic in the morning when he could not find his keys to go to work the next day. I have always needed to be in an environment of Peace, Love, and Harmony. This introspective, closer look into who I really am is life-transforming. It is also very much about a love story with myself. It's about how I can truly love and care for "ME" as much as I do for others. I am a work in progress and this work has been a lifelong journey. I have more work to do; however, I know *who* I am, *whose* I am, and I love and respect who I am becoming.

Introspection is a very critical element of our overall growth and development. Introspection is the examination of our own conscious thoughts and feelings. In my research into psychology, I learned that the process of introspection relies exclusively on observation of one's mental state. In a spiritual realm, introspection refers to the examination of one's soul. You must prioritize examining your own conscious thoughts and feelings. I invest a considerable amount of time examining my own stuff. I stay in my head ... a lot. Such introspection can be good. There are times when such effort can be detrimental. If you write in your diary after an unhappy break-up, you are being introspective. *Introspicere* means "to look inside." This is metaphorically what an introspective person does. As I "introspect" and reflect on my life, I seem to always write out my thoughts and feelings. I really did not know at the time what I was doing, but I knew I had to express everything on paper. I realized I was journaling. Journaling has been an amazingly effective tool for me. The vast majority of my hardships are written in journals. Not long ago, as I was wading through some boxes to purge things from my life, I ran across several journals from the time my son was born through the death of my mother, my father, my sister Kathi, and even my beloved dog, Ebony. If this is something you do not do, I strongly encourage and urge you to write and express yourself, even if just to you. In my research, I found the Introspective Personality as a concept. And although it may be difficult at times to really look at ourselves and examine what part we played in our situation and our life's circumstances, it is extremely necessary. And be clear, you are not trying to make yourself wrong; you are simply uncovering "YOU." There is so much significance to our thoughts and actions. If we accept and learn from these thoughts and actions, if we take note of our mistakes or missteps, the lessons learned, and our triumphs, yes, we have those too, we increase our self-awareness, we become free. As famed author Maya Angelou notes, "the caged bird/sings of freedom." Through your introspective personality, glean so many valuable insights that you'll set yourself free. Be Free!

I truly believe that the time I spend alone in thought can be positive. That quiet time creates a rich environment for personal growth and creativity. It can, however, also be very concerning when we are negatively turned against ourselves. I am sure you have often heard that thoughts are things and are powerful beyond words. Introspection can be a process of healthy self-reflection, examination, and exploration, which is good for your well-being and your brain. However, we must be careful and mindful.

Often you are forced into introspection; at least, I know that is true for me. Life happens, and sometimes, many times, life is Good, but often it does not feel good. It is often said that "Bad things happen to good people." And when I really take a good honest look inside, it brings out my Truth. This is when I actually see and recognize my True Blessings in Disguise. I have so many stories and examples that have pushed me into the Introspective realm of living. When I reflect, despite what happened or transpired that looked or felt wrong, I always end up on top, as it relates to my Truth. Some people may mean it for bad or to be hurtful, but I know GOD always means it for GOOD. If I just wait on it, Good is revealed, it is unleashed, and often in very visible and tangible ways.

Let me share one story about an experience that tossed me into a deep introspective look at my life. I learned who I really was as a person and a professional. These life events expose you for who you are and unveil your strength and conviction in this life. Imagine this: You've worked very hard all your adult life. You've finished undergraduate studies and graduate school with two degrees in hand. You've struggled to manage your life as a single parent. You've worked hard to make something of yourself. You desire to be an example to your one and only child. That was me. I'd held leadership and management positions most of my career. I'd been blessed to steadily move up the career ladder over the years. I was able to propel myself into a pretty prestigious professional position as a State Director.

That year, I relocated from Los Angeles, California, to another state to serve as the State Director for a well-known Federal Program. I was hired to help turn around a struggling program plagued with fraud and upper management challenges that were not uncommon for this state, this department, and this program. They had struggled for decades. The Department had new strong executive leadership and a goal to turn this program around. I was recruited, hired, and charged with transforming the State program and staff. It was a tall order, but I had faith in my abilities and the team that I would assemble. Over my four+ year tenure, we transformed the program from the worst program to being one of the best in the nation—a complete about face. My team and I received accolades, compliments, and praise from local, state, and federal entities. They acknowledged the great work we had accomplished. We were respected and appreciated for our hard work and dedication. The program team was praised for bringing positive life and light to this State program.

Well, in the fall of my fourth year, things dramatically changed for me when a new division director was hired. Prior to that, there was a fallout and shifting of my superiors, and at this time, there was an interim Director of my division for a little over a year. All was well, and my team worked well with this individual. However, instead of that person being hired into the actual Director position, a new outside individual was hired—someone with neither knowledge or experience in this particular program nor its history. No idea from which we came. My job became increasingly uncomfortable. I was harassed and belittled by this individual. I had not experienced such behavior from a supervisor over the course of my 45+ year career. I began to feel I was being pushed out, or they were creating the conditions for someone to take over. Less than three months of being there, this individual went so far as to give me a written "Final Warning" letter. Final warning, are you hearing this? The letter included multiple accusations of my poor work performance and unprofessional behavior. That was insane. I had never received verbal warnings or written performance letters from any of my directors over the course of my four years there, nor in my entire professional career, which spans four decades. I received nothing but rave performance feedback from my supervisors. They were completely satisfied with my progress. I continually received positive comments, feedback, and high accolades for my work. Not to say that I thought I was a perfect person, but not even close to what this individual was making me out to be. Again from the Department Executive leaders to local and national Offices, and from management to colleagues and others, my work and the work of my team was highly regarded. The Commissioner of this government department openly and often chanted, "The Program is Fixed."

I was certainly open to improving my practice; however, it is disingenuous to receive a performance write-up without any notice. What was even more disconcerting was the stance of the executive leadership team. We had worked extremely well together over the years. They were appreciative and supportive of me. It suddenly felt like they were allowing these actions to take place unchecked. It was crushing because if there had been any concerns, they had not been expressed with me. This was a devastating and stressful experience. It was truly unlike anything I had encountered. This was discrimination, and I could not tell you exactly why. I still cannot; however, I know what discrimination feels like, and it is terrible.

While I did not know all that was going on, I felt my job was at risk. I really did not know where to turn. The Human Resource Director within the organization said I needed to look outside the organization because I did not have any recourse given my high level within the department. I took his advice. After 45+ years of employment, I was in new territory. I retained an attorney who assisted me with preparing a proposal and requested an exit package. I figured this made sense because it was clear the organization no longer valued me or my skills. The program was where it needed to be. The Department was redeemed nationally. I did what I was hired to do, so I figured this was their way of letting me go. Of course, they flatly declined my proposal. We then filed an Equal Opportunity Commission (EOC) claim for age discrimination. I was 63 years young and on the heels of retirement. As an African-American and a woman, I thought my claim would be a triple threat. I could just move on.

As the claim progressed and the harassment continued, I felt incredible internal stresses. All of this was so challenging; I didn't understand it. It took a toll on me and adversely affected my health. I was nearly hospitalized, and my physician immediately took me off work. I was off work for about three months on Family Medical Leave. That was very difficult for me because I would never have taken off work were it not for my physician directing me otherwise. I am not a quitter. I refused to let them see what I sensed and what I felt. Of course, my body told my story for free. I hated that it had given out on me.

Although the EOC claim was still in process, I returned to work in good faith. I was hoping to get past it all. I worked for seven days. During those days, things still felt uncomfortable for me. I could sense something brewing. It was as if they didn't expect me to return. I felt they wanted me to be an "Angry Black Woman" and quit. I was diligent and worked hard during that period of time.

My supervisor seemed upset by my decision to file a claim. I didn't have any other choice. I was being treated unfairly. Unbeknown to me, there was a secret investigation occurring with my team by the Office of Inspector General (OIG) that week I was back. Secretly something was up. They insinuated that my team had violated a finance policy during a meeting that was held about five months prior. It all seemed so calculated. They were looking for something on me. But my record was clean, so they targeted my staff. I then was called to meet with the OIG on a Friday at the end of the workday. They were cryptic throughout the meeting. They told me my team violated a financial policy to the tune of $1,666. Mind you, my overall budget was nearly $300 million. They would not tell me how my team violated it. They would not share any details. As the director, I didn't get a chance to conduct my own investigation into what was or was not done. My immediate Director neither discussed this matter with me that day nor was it mentioned, discussed, or written in the final warning writeup. This was interesting since that allegedly occurred before the writeup, yet there was no mention of it in the writeup. It just came out of nowhere, it was all a surprise. I left the office that afternoon, right after that meeting with OIG. I had lots on my mind. What was really going on? Why were they so secretive? What was my team thinking? Why were these competent people being harassed and pulled into this situation? Clearly, it was all targeted at me.

Now this meeting occurred on a Friday afternoon, and remember, I had only been back to work from my leave of absence one week. That upcoming Monday, I had a follow-up appointment with my doctor, so I had previously requested the day off. I was ready to get back to work on Tuesday so I could get an understanding of all that had transpired and get to the bottom of it. A Human Resources staffer called me at home that day and told me that "I" was terminated for violating the Employee Group Meals and Healthy Meeting Policy. "Please do not return to the office. We will deliver a box to you. Please use it to return all Department property." I stared at the phone with a good blend of shock and relief. I was shocked by my unfair dismissal. I was oddly relieved to be removed from such a toxic culture and climate. While I would miss close colleagues and my awesome team, I would not miss the hostile work environment.

As things unfolded, the EOC reached a decision about my age discrimination after my termination. They did not rule in my favor. I was advised, however, to file a retaliation claim since I'd been terminated. I was told that was unfair practice while in the middle of an ECO Claim.

That began a year-long journey in pursuit of justice. As I reflect on it all, I know my ego was the driving force. I thought, "How could they get away with this injustice?" I was relentless. It was a struggle, a battle I could not win. A dear friend reminded me that even though this doesn't make any sense, I am trying to make something logical out of an illogical situation. Yep, he was right.

I had to remind myself of the truth, God's Truth. I had to get away from my ego. I had to remember who and whose I am. Once I began the process of introspection, I opened my eyes to this ultimate Blessing in Disguise. My reputation as a consummate professional extended beyond the confines of this organization. My work ethic and reputation were highly regarded locally and nationally. What was I trying to prove? Why was I stressing over this and letting my situation make me ill?

Once I got still, I realized ego had taken over. I needed to kick it out of that situation and out of my life. I promised God I would nix the ego. I would release the situation to my high power. I would move on with my life. I would stop seeking legal advice. I would stop talking about the matter. I have so much more to me and so much more to give. I was brought there to transform the State program, and I did. I left behind the most awesome team of people. I was no longer needed. I fulfilled my mission. Right then, I made a choice to move forward with my life. No sooner than I completed that promise in the form of a prayer, God swiftly moved on my behalf.

I grew up hearing "God don't like ugly" and "Payback is a b*tch." Those who had plotted and planned my termination and many of those who stood on the sidelines complacent as my work was dismantled were eventually fired. They lost positions within the department and with other organizations they may have moved to. Not because of me, but because of a direct reflection of who they really were. The universe simply caught up with them. Karma. I do believe in Karma. Need I say more?

Over the years since this situation, I have continued to lean on my faith, use the tools in this book, and tap into my support system to live my best life ever. I only tell this story for you to know that life happens and it is working for us. I wasted valuable time challenging this situation, and I understand our humanness will take us there. But if you take the time to go within and reflect, you will see your Blessings in Disguise.

I recommend you proactively complete this Introspective exercise below before you are pushed to do it. Also, know it's a tool when you need it. Trust me, life will happen and force you to take a step back and reflect. If we do not take the time for ourselves, nothing will change. When one steps in courageously and intentionally, we grow and unfold in a way you may have never thought possible.

Do this exercise as often as you need or desire. You can do this on something very specific that you may be dealing with or in general for your livelihood. Knowing and understanding yourself is another powerful ritual that I strongly advise. The aim here is for you to begin to know yourself. Keep in mind this can come in many forms such as Self-Talk and Internal dialogue; through this process, you will most likely uncover known or unknown fears, barriers, and blockages. Always remember you are an expert, yes you are, you are an Expert on "YOU." Make sure you are clear about this. No one knows you better than you know yourself. Others may make you second guess what you know, but at the end of the day, you know "YOU." Introspections will bring this Truth to the forefront and to the Light; you will begin to live your Truth. And living your Truth is being free—the best feeling in the world.

The Introspection Exercise

Start small and do your best to build the ritual of introspection exercise into your life.

1. Find or Create a Quiet Space. It could be somewhere in your home, or I often go to the beach or a peaceful venue. Water soothes me. I can be open and receptive to my thoughts.
2. When you are there, be sure to always take a moment, take a full conscious breath (breathing in for 6 to 8 seconds then hold for 4 to 6 seconds (longer if you can) and then release the breath (exhale) completely for a 6- to 8-second count). I recommend you do at least three full deep breaths before you get started in your exercise. Focus on your breathing throughout this process. This will keep you in the present; spiritually speaking, it is your connection with GOD.
3. Begin to Ask Deep, Open-Ended Questions. Now that you've created this space for yourself See What Comes Up with No Judgment.

4. Take Notes.
5. Reflect and Repeat if needed.
6. What Comes Up for you?

Complete the information below or use your Personal Action Plan in Chapter Two. You can complete something like this below, or create your own:

As a result of my Introspection exercise today, I will be ...
  Starting ...

Continuing ...

THE S.P.I.C.E. OF LIFE

Stopping ...

_____

_____

_____

_____

_____

_____

_____

_____

THE WINNING TRINITY EXERCISE

When I facilitate workshops, I often ask, "What does your name say are your social virtues or values for life?" Introspection can often reveal to you your personal Winning Trinity in Life. Even though this exercise is fun to do, I truly believe that what comes up for you is not a coincidence; seek to find out why this came up for you and what you need to learn from it, or what you are supposed to help others with. They usually come up because you need them or you have the expertise to help others. Here is an example of this activity using each letter of my first and last names:

Debra = Determination, Excellence, Builds, Renunciation, Awareness

Lynn = Loyal, Youthful, Nice, Nuanced

Keyes = Kindness, Enthusiasm, Yield, Effort, Self-discipline

THE S.P.I.C.E. OF LIFE

1. Awareness, Appreciative, Ambitious
2. Builds, Believe, Best
3. Clarity, Courage Compassion
4. Desires, Determination, Dedication
5. Excellence, Enthusiasm, Effort
6. Faith, Focus, Foster
7. Gifts, Goals, Grateful
8. Honest, Humility, Hunger
9. Intelligence, Integrity, Imagination
10. Justice, Joyfulness, Joy
11. Keys, Kindness, Knowledge
12. Loyalty, Law, Love
13. Motivation, Mindfulness, Mindset
14. Nirvana, New, Nice
15. Obedience, Optimum, Orderliness
16. Prayerful, Purposefulness, Powerful
17. Quality, Quiet, Quantity
18. Reliability, Responsibility, Resilience
19. Self-disciplined, Steadfast, Spiritual
20. Trustworthy, Truthful, Thankful
21. Universal, Unifying, Understanding
22. Vision, Victorious, Validity
23. Wondrous, Will, Willingness
24. Xenial, Xenacious, X-factor
25. Youthful, Yield, Yes
26. Zeal, Zealous, Zion

THE S.P.I.C.E. OF LIFE

Here is an example of this activity using only the first letter of someone's name and using a different list of positive attributes and traits:

Patrick = Prayerful, Purposefulness, Powerful

These values may be important in your daily living. Identify three to five values that stand out and make you smile or really resonate within you. What can you do each day to BE the values you've chosen? When you do this, you will end each day with an attitude of gratitude. It becomes the perfect closing, despite what else transpired that day.

THE S.P.I.C.E. OF LIFE

THE S.P.I.C.E. OF LIFE

Introspection Lessons Learned

Write your thoughts about these:

Does Introspection fit in my life? If it does, where and how does it fit? If it doesn't, share your thoughts.

_____

_____

_____

What is one Introspection Practice that I will START now that will benefit my life's journey?

_____

_____

_____

What is one Introspection Practice that I will KEEP using because it has consistently worked for me?

_____

_____

_____

What is one Introspection Practice that I must STOP because it is not for my best and highest good?

_____

_____

THE S.P.I.C.E. OF LIFE

As I reflect on Introspection, what do I believe?

As I reflect on Introspection, what do I know?

What is my affirmation for my Introspection? What is my overall goal?

What are some Divine Nurturing Words of comfort and peace for Introspection?

THE S.P.I.C.E. OF LIFE

My Introspection Story

Reflect on your life and think about your Introspection Story. Did your childhood—or an experience—form or shape your introspection. If either did, how so? Use this space to write your Introspection Story. You may consider your thoughts from "Introspection: Lessons Learned" to help you write your story.

THE S.P.I.C.E. OF LIFE

THE S.P.I.C.E. OF LIFE

NOTES ON INTROSPECTION

Conscious Connections

CONSCIOUS CONNECTIONS

Conscious Connections may be a concept that is new to many. Having a mindful conscious connection with everything in life puts you in a state of awareness. Consciousness is defined as the state of being awake and aware of one's surroundings. I take this even further and say it is being attuned to developing a Conscious Connection mindset to all aspects of your life. This is life-changing. When you slow down and take time to give the proper attention to everything you do, you will expand the insight and knowledge that will protect you. You begin to see how all aspects of life work together for one's best and highest good. The result is taking control over your life versus life taking control over you. In this chapter, I have selected a few areas to focus on. They have enhanced my life tremendously. Once you grasp the concept of beginning to exercise conscious connections within your daily living, you intuitively connect with all of life. It becomes second nature. A few areas to focus on include but are not limited to our words, thoughts and feelings, relationships, food and nourishments, money and finance, and even gratitude.

Connections simply means the action of linking one thing to another. People move about by routine and habits blindly without even thinking about what we are doing or what we are thinking. When we do this, unintended things happen. In this case, connecting our focus and attention, our conscious mind, to aspects of our life helps us to function and move and have our being with intention. By doing this, we are not led or pulled by outside circumstances, voices, or experiences. For example, I broke my elbow or fell down stairs because I was not consciously connected to what I was doing. I was not aware of my surroundings, or what I was wearing. It means paying attention. Being conscious about your words, your thoughts, and those feelings will make a difference in the outcome of situations and circumstances that arise in life. Do you want to be conscious about the food you eat? Do you want to be conscious about the relationships that you have? I'd say yes.

I became stronger in my connections and consciously focused on being attuned to that which made a significant impact in my world, my life, and how I chose to live it. Although I have only selected a few to expand on, one can look at many different aspects and parts of our existence where we really do not consciously pay attention. We take them for granted. For example, our body and how it functions. We have so much control over our health and physical wellness, from the simple to the complex, from our feet and toes to our hands and fingers. We all know how we feel when we have a seemingly small accident like stumping your toe. It causes the worst pain you can imagine and can slow you down for weeks. Ahh, my toes are an important part of this machine we call our body.

Being conscious of the words you use, the thoughts you think, and the feelings you experience is your gateway, your path through life. What this means is that when you consciously and intentionally move through life—making connections with everything you do and everyone you meet—life will not just happen to you, but rather you will be aware of life. This is the awareness that builds clarity in your life. No surprises, no confusion, no "I was not aware that if I did that, it would affect me in this way" … none of this! Your purposeful consciousness will reveal the facts that will guide you to making the right decisions. Knowing and completely understanding this allowed me to be in control, and I was able to make informed decisions for myself. I learned at a very young age and became a strong believer that what you think about and what you speak about, you bring about in your world. Hands Down! Please trust me about this one! I learned, "I am the thinker, who thinks the thoughts, who creates my experiences." I have created many experiences in my mind, good or not so good.

I have often said things and spoken in ways that may not have been my truth. I knew those words were not what I believed. However, because of low self-esteem and not having confidence in myself, I often spoke untruths. Bam! It would come to pass. Once I acknowledged my Truth, embraced my Truth, and spoke my Truth, I began living in my Truth. I am sure you have done it from time to time, if not all the time. Saying things like, "I can't," "I am not ready," or "I won't," yet knowing full well you could, would, and that you are ready. All you had to do was tell yourself and then believe it. We all have different reasons for these crazy thought processes. Maybe a parent, close friend, a teacher, or society told you you were not ready, or not good enough, or would never measure up to anything. So you believed it and lived your life accordingly. We are sometimes afraid of speaking our Truth, and when you speak words out loud to the universe, the conscious mind hears and provides you with whatever you believe is true. American industrialist, Henry Ford, is noted for sharing this truth: "Whether you think you can or you think you can't, you're right." There are dozens of sayings and poems that speak to this. I especially love a poem by *Walter D. Wintle*. One day while in a salon with Ron, my friend and hairdresser, I confided in him how much I needed to stay on top of what I say, think, and believe. He recited this poem from memory. It was meaningful and powerful:

"If you think you are beaten, you are
If you think you dare not, you don't,
If you like to win, but you think you can't
It is almost certain you won't.

If you think you'll lose, you're lost
For out of the world we find,
Success begins with a fellow's will
It's all in the state of mind.

If you think you are outclassed, you are
You've got to think high to rise,
You've got to be sure of yourself before
You can ever win a prize.

Life's battles don't always go

THE S.P.I.C.E. OF LIFE

To the stronger or faster man,
But soon or late the man who wins
Is the man WHO THINKS HE CAN!"[1]

It may take a little time and practice, but becoming connected with your words, thoughts, and feelings and then making effective and conscious changes will become a ritual, something that you do without thinking a lot. It will become a part of who you are. You become unconsciously competent. In psychology, there are four stages of competence expressed in the Conscious Competence Learning Model. When you begin to make these shifts in your consciousness, you want them to become "Unconscious Competence." Let me explain why this is so powerful.

The Conscious Competence Learning Model first used by Martin M. Broadwell in 1969 and further developed by Noel Burch in the 1970s, is based on the premise that before a learning experience begins, learners are unaware of what or how much they know (unconscious incompetence), and as they learn, they move through psychological states until they reach a stage of unconscious competence. By understanding the four-stage model, and the different stages you are in, you can better identify where you are and how you can make yourself completely competent and; therefore, you will do the right things without even trying. To break it down further, it is important to be clear that while the words, thoughts, and

---

[1] Originally published in "Unity" 1905 edition by Unity Tract Society, Unity School of Christianity.

feelings may come from your own mind, often they come from others who plant a seed that you allow to be planted in your mind. And if you are not careful and conscious or mindful, you'll take them on, water them, and cause them to grow. You will actually believe something that you know is not true for you or your situation.

1. **Unconscious Incompetence:** In unconscious incompetence, we are not aware that a skill or knowledge gap exists. We do not know what we do not know. Therefore until you become aware of something, you'll never do anything. If someone does not know there is a problem, they are less likely to engage in the solution.

2. **Conscious Incompetence:** In conscious incompetence, we are aware of a skill or knowledge gap and understand the importance of acquiring the new skill or obtaining the information. It is in this stage that changes can begin.

3. **Conscious Competence:** In conscious competence, we know how to use the skill or the knowledge. We know how to perform the task. Doing these require action, practice, conscious thought, and hard work to be competent and consistent.

4. **Unconscious Competence:** In unconscious competence, we have had enough experience with the skill that we can perform it so easily, consistently, and we do it unconsciously.

THE S.P.I.C.E. OF LIFE

Conscious connection will get you to a place where you will subconsciously seek words that uplift you, empower you, and that speak to your real heart's desires. Here is an A to Z look at some inspiring and uplifting words, phrases, and feelings. Take time and come up with some of your own.

Consider using words, thoughts, phrases, and feelings that create higher vibrations in your life. Notice the difference and power in these little _Shifts_ in words, phrases, and thoughts from A to Z.

Act as if you have or are **versus** Don't have/can't have/you are not. Be what you want to achieve in life.

But + positive statement **versus** But + a negative statement. BUT will cancel out what you say before it. For example, "I think you did a good job, but next time you could move faster" versus "I think next time you could move faster BUT you did a great job."

Clarity and understanding **versus** Confused or lack of understanding. Speak what you want to experience. So instead of saying, "I am confused," you say, "I seek to be clear" or "I seek to understand."

Did for me **versus** Did to me—you don't want to be a victim.

Expect **versus** Hope, Hoping is nice to have, and Expecting shows your conviction and power.

THE S.P.I.C.E. OF LIFE

Faith it until you make it **versus** Fake it until you make.

Growing through **versus** Going through. Whatever is happening you will be better because of it.

Have to **versus** Get to (or choose to). Always remember your Blessing in all things.

It's When **versus** If. Stay focused on your goal, whatever it is.

Just is a word that minimizes you and your truth. Simply say cancel cancel or delete delete to anything you say or think is not for your best and highest good. Be firm and confident in your truth.

Keep your head high, know your worth. Be proud and always hold your head up.

Learn to use your "Yes" and "No" for your best and highest Good, not others. There is power in using both.

Manage your energy and your time. There is power in Energy Management, please learn.

Nurture and protect your inner-self. That is a God-given gift we often forget we have.

THE S.P.I.C.E. OF LIFE

Or **versus** And. You don't always have to limit yourself, you can do both, so do not give up on your dreams. Focus on your "WHY" and then your "HOW" will emerge.

Practice using high vibrational words and phrases. When someone tells you thank you for your service, you say "No problem" or "No worries." Although you meant well, the person may think you thought of them as a potential problem or worrisome. However, respond how you learned as a young child, and say, "You are welcome." That phrase is a higher vibrational phrase.

Quitting is not an option. Making a conscious change or shift in plans is perfectly fine. Usually people will quit because they don't believe in themselves; they are worried or afraid. Never give up on your dreams, whatever they may be.

Realize the way we give up our power is by thinking we do not have any power. You have the power.

Shift **versus** Stuck. When you feel you are stuck, all that is needed is to make a small shift in thought, in direction, or plans.

True affirming statements **versus** Try. Trying is basically saying you will not. It keeps you in a state of trying. You want to affirm what you will do. When you put it out there that is what you will most likely do, saying "try" is a way out. Be authentic. "Yes, I will be there," or "No, I will not be there." Certainly things might change, and if you can't make it after all, you let them know as soon as you know for sure. And if you are able to go when you said you were not, it will be a pleasant surprise.

Understand. Dr. Stephen Covey reminded us that "many people do not listen with the intent to understand, they listen with the intent to reply." Seek to Understand by listening. This is the foundation of communication.

Victor **versus** Victim. Don't allow yourself to be a victim. Always be victorious because it makes you wiser. When something occurs we might be the victim first, but never twice.

Wronged **versus** Blessing in Disguise. Seek your Blessing in all things and all circumstances. It's there!

Xerox, copy, or duplicate what is good in your life.

You **versus** I. Pay attention to when to use each.

Zip and zap. Move at high speed, compressing energy vigor **versus** a Sudden burst of energy that makes a dramatic impact.

Conscious Connection with relationships includes people, places, or things. All relationships are vital and are necessary in life for us to thrive. People, places, and things are in our lives for a reason, a season, or a lifetime. That is the reason we must cultivate them, no matter the purpose.

We all have a variety of relationships. While many are healthy, some may be challenged. There is compelling evidence that strong relationships and bonds contribute to long healthy, happy, and fulfilling lives. The relationships we form with others are key to our mental and emotional wellbeing. They are essential to our survival.

First of all, let's look at who or what our relations are with—family, friends, partnerships in love, business, and pets—and we even have relationships with things and places. We are in relationships every day, all day—even with ourselves. If you really think about it, our relationship with ourselves is the most important. All relationships are necessary and essential to our existence. If a relationship does not work out or last long, consider its purpose is no longer needed in your life. This is not always a bad thing. Often it is good, as it means you are fulfilled and can move on to a bigger and better you. All relationships are successful, based on how you view them. Some no longer serve you emotionally, spiritually, or functionally. They all have or had good redeeming qualities, at least at some point. We must focus on these qualities. Think about how —regardless of the outcome of a relationship—you grew from the experience. We always gain insight, knowledge, skills, and strength from them. Even if the relationship is still going strong, you are growing into the person you want to be because of it. All of this is something I needed to learn. It took me a long time. Class is still in session, because it is a lifelong endeavor. I am thankful for all of my past relationships as well as all of my current ones. They are serving me at this very moment as I am on this current path. In truth, they all served a powerful purpose in my life and my journey.

When we think about certain relationships that we think failed, we feel we lost something. Nelson Mandela noted, "I never lose, I either win or I learn." So very true! You stand in your power. The feeling of loss can be turned around to seeing that loss actually leads to your gain. This is another example of your Blessing in Disguise.

We all strive to maintain a conscious connection with GOD, whatever that means to you. Most believe there is a higher power at work in our lives. However, we often struggle with our understanding and our connections. In the first chapter we discussed that a Spiritual practice is any regular and intentional activity that helps us nourish and strengthen our personal relationship and conscious connection with our Divine self. It brings balance to our lives. I encourage you to create and use your own list of Spiritual Practices. We are individuals, and you must individualize the practices that work for us.

I believe that the main key components to healthy relationships is to master five things: talk, listen to understand, communicate openly, trust, and have genuine respect in any type of relationship. Although we have many different relationships in our lives—with people, animals, places, circumstances, and things—my focus here is our relationships with people. As humans, we all have an acquired thought process and we have our own unique take on life. We have these thoughts that are constantly active in our minds, in our consciousness. They create what I call internal self-talk. Only the person can hear it, in their head.

Here is a great example of what can happen when one or more of these components are missing. Individuals create their own personal inner self talk narrative to the same situation. Let's take a story about Donald and Betty. They were introduced about eight months ago through mutual friends. They hit it off great; they had a lot in common. They got along wonderfully well in the beginning. They spent a lot of quality time together. One day while just walking on the beach on a beautiful day, Betty—basking in the moment—blurted out, "Wow, we have been dating now for almost eight months." Donald, while thoroughly enjoying his time with Betty on the beach, did not respond right away. He smiled, though, but then had this concerning look on his face. This is when their self-talk began:

Betty is saying to herself, "Oh, he has nothing to say, I probably should not have said that. He is probably not ready for a serious talk and he thinks I am being pushy. But heck, I have the right to express my feelings. Maybe he doesn't really like me. I mean he is not all that anyway. I really don't need him; I don't really need a man. Heck, we can just go back to the car and he can take me home. I have been through this before, I know the signs. We do not ever have to talk again. Because I am going to say what I want. I don't need him to agree or to think he is rescuing me."

At the same time, Donald is saying to himself, "Wow she is right, I must really like this woman. She is so sweet and easy to be with.

Not to mention beautiful and foxy. How did I get so lucky ... eight months ... Wait, has it been eight months? Man, I am overdue to get my car serviced. It needs an oil change. The last time I neglected taking care of that, my car engine died. And that cost me a pretty penny."

Betty finally spoke up, "You know, never mind, I am sorry I said anything. I don't need you. I don't need to be saved. I don't need a man in shining armor to ride up on a white horse to save me. Let's just go back to the car and you can take me home."

As they walked back, Donald looked at her very puzzled, wondering if he missed something. He drove her home, no words spoken between the two of them. They pulled up to her house and she said, "Bye!" and jumped from the car, slamming the door. She walked away and never looked back. She went into her house, called her best friend, and began to tell her horrible story—the one she had created in her head.

Donald looked dumbfounded and said nothing. He let her jump out of the car and run into her house. He wanted to stop her and ask her if she was okay and what had brought all that on? He drove home, went inside, got a couple of beers out of his refrigerator, and kicked back in his easy chair to watch the basketball game. He felt a little weird about what happened. They were having such a nice day. Maybe she was just going through something. Maybe she will call to let him in on what was going on. A couple of days later, he saw his friend who had introduced them. The friend asked, "So, how are things going with you and

THE S.P.I.C.E. OF LIFE

Betty?" Donald looked at his friend, shrugged his shoulders and asked, "Do you know anything about a white horse?"

This is a funny, yet realistic example of how our thoughts—the seeds we plant in our mind—can grow into our own narratives. All of this represents what my friend calls Stinking Thinking (ST). ST can play a detrimental role in our life experiences and in our relationships if we are not careful. I have a very dear friend and mentor, Marlene, who would say, "Ok, stop! You need to change that narrative" anytime I would go to her with my pitiful stuff. When I stop and change the narrative, it all falls in Divine order. I have learned to only plant the seeds I desire to grow.

Moments of Stinking Thinking are often lacking the basic relationship tenet: TLC. And no, this is not what you think it is! One of the most important things I truly believe is a key ingredient in healthy relationships is what I have coined a TLC. What comes to mind when you see the acronym TLC? Maybe you have no idea at all. And if you can think of something, it's most likely Tender Loving Care. Am I right? As I define it, TLC means TALK, LISTEN, COMMUNICATE. It is about TLC with others and—more importantly—with yourself and with GOD. This is a clever take on Talk, Listen and Communicate. These are the keys that open and sustain strong relationships, essential to our existence. Wouldn't you agree? Think about it. We must be able to relate to and communicate with everybody. Whether we have been searching for love all of our life or just beginning to search for our soul mate, or maybe you have found "the one" and are struggling with your choice, the Key Ingredient tips in this chapter bring awareness and insight that guarantee success. Although this chapter focuses on Relationships—as in finding or sustaining the right and perfect soul mate—the concepts apply to all relationships such as parent and child, employees, co-workers and bosses, and friends and acquaintances. Everything is based on relationships! Once you understand and become clear about how to develop, build, and nurture your relationships, you will become stronger and confident in attracting the right and perfect relationships you desire.

"Our word is our bond." Regardless of what that word is, it will be true for you. "What you believe you will achieve" and "It is done to you as you believe" are some of the quotations and sayings that remind us of this truth. Faith yields belief, and belief yields knowing. Knowingness is the ultimate truth. To achieve this Truth you must Talk, you must Listen, and you must genuinely Communicate. This is lacking in most of our relationships. As what happened in our little story, Betty and Donald did not talk openly to each other in this instance. They let the relationship go to where their inner thoughts were taking them. No discussion was taking place. When the conversation started, they did not know how to have a healthy exchange of communication.

If asked, "What is the most important element in any relationship?," what would you say? This can be asked of any relationship—couples, children, mothers, fathers, coworkers. Before you even think about it, you would most likely say Communication. Right? I would like to give a different thought process. While Communication is important, it is not the answer I'm seeking. Some may have even said Love. I would not argue with that. However, when speaking in general terms, there may not be love associated with all relationships, like relationships with coworkers and bosses. Love would have greater importance in familial relationships, although Love is not really necessary at all. The ultimate element that results from TLC is developing a clear understanding of expectations. What?!? Where did that come from? I've got you wondering now. Yep, when we know and seek to understand each other in any given situation or circumstances, we all win. This is a piece that is often left out. The clarity of our expectations of each other and ourselves is critical. The only way you can uncover this, the only way you can truly communicate, is that you must talk with and listen to each other. You are talking with and listening to better understand each other. My experience has been that when this is lacking in any relationship, it may lead in the wrong direction and break ups or break downs, and severed relationships most likely will result. Let's talk about the Talking and Listening Skills:

Talking is an essential key to building a strong relationship. We must learn to speak to each other to let our thoughts and feelings and concerns be known. Often, we keep our thoughts to ourselves, expecting others to read our minds. Maybe we are afraid to speak up, maybe we want to keep the peace. Talking in and of itself is not the issue. It is more of what we don't say or more importantly what we say and how we say it, and even the actions that accompany it. If you are coming off aggressive, mean, or mad, you can turn the other party off from hearing you. We must be able to assess how we talk to people. Then we can determine what changes may be needed to get our points across. Or is it even necessary to get our point across? When you talk negatively about the person, you bring more of that type of person or the behavior to your life. If you say loving and positive things, you will attract that back to you. In all instances, you must talk about your expectations. It is better to sort them out up front than to have something come up later down the line. You have to talk it out. Sometimes you can do this on your own; other times, you may need special assistance. If you truly want a resolution, or a solid connection, you have to do what you have to do, TALK. When seeking a mate, find someone who is open to this.

Listening: Seems simple enough, right? Wrong. This is one of the biggest areas of breakdown in relationship-building. Listening is key. Most of us would say we are good listeners. But are you? Do you listen to hear what is being said? Or are you only listening to determine how you are going to respond, what you will say to defend your position? Are you preparing your response, rebuttal, or defense? We do listen, but do we really hear? Yes, HEAR! This part of listening is still something many do not possess. Taking time to see how effective you listen to really hear the person and what they are saying is a skill recommended to assess and to master. It involves learning to be a reflective listener. Hearing makes all the difference in the world. It is as simple as saying, "Let me make sure I hear and understand what you are saying. You said XYZ, is that correct?" This gives the person a chance to clarify, if needed. And your response can then be appropriate. If they were talking about apples and oranges and you thought they mentioned something altogether different, so you responded about broccoli, they would think you were not even listening and might be irritated. There are many Active Listening activities and trainings worth researching. It's an important skill to develop.

Communication: Is communication the ultimate goal or result? We must know how to communicate with ourselves and with others. Once you have truly talked and truly listened, you are now communicating. You will communicate your understanding of each other's expectations and how you will navigate through any differences. Communication gets you to a level of complete understanding and appreciation of the other person. This exercise makes way for a successful relationship. Through this process, though, you may find that it is not a good match; you cannot agree on expectations. It is best to know that now, rather than going down a road of doom or unhappiness. Should you decide to work through things, then constant communication is necessary—communicating daily, which includes talking, listening, and hearing. When we strive to understand and care for each other, you win. You will not be guessing or wondering. You will make expectations clear, then honor or revisit them when needed. Together, these essential Communications skills (TLC, Talk, Listen, Communicate) yield Tender Loving Care (TLC), which is our ultimate goal.

Let's take a moment to look at your fears, blockage, and barriers. When taking time to reflect, you are looking inwards. You are dropping down deep in the depth of your being. Learning what triggered you can help to build two components of your being—self-awareness and self-regulation. Self-awareness gives you the ability to understand your emotions, strengths, weaknesses, drives, values and goals, and recognize their impact on you and others. If what comes up needs to be addressed or if fear, blocks, or barriers seem to be holding you down or back, use the "Conquering Fears, Blocks or Barriers" exercise. Self-regulation comes into play here. You can take what comes up and begin to work on controlling your behaviors, thoughts, and habits that are causing those feelings and changing into a better brighter outlook on life events. You may want to work with a personal or spiritual coach or professional counselor. Sometimes we need that, and it is nothing to be ashamed of. Some very deep emotions and feelings may come up. Please work with a professional, if needed. This exercise is very rewarding if you open up and let the process work. This exercise is helpful to do before you begin to make your Personal Action Plan.

THE S.P.I.C.E. OF LIFE

It's important to create a space where you can gain mastery over obstacles or oppositions, and where you can control your own self-talk. When we feel like we want to quit, to give up, or throw in the towel, it is usually because we are experiencing fears, blockages, or barriers. Conquering these will help you gain the mental and moral power to overcome them. This is done by creating affirmations about your TRUTH. Take the time to meditate on each section before writing your response. Once you have created your Affirmation, say it every day, three times a day, for at least 30 days, or until you have owned and embodied it and conquered that fear, blockage, or barrier.

CONQUERING FEARS, BLOCKAGES, AND BARRIERS WORKSHEET

My Fear, Blockage, or Barrier is:

_____

_____

The Root cause of My Fear, Blockage, or Barrier is:

_____

_____

The TRUTH is:

_____

_____

My AFFIRMATION is:

_____

_____

THE S.P.I.C.E. OF LIFE

FOOD CONNECTIONS
MINDFUL EATING

We typically think of conscious connection with thoughts, words, and people. I think it is equally important to consider such connections with our health. For example, let's consider food. What we eat has a connection with consciousness, because food is tied to the brain. When we do not have quality nutrients entering the body, we significantly imbalance the brain—the part of the brain that really needs proper nutrition to function. Zen Master and global spiritual leader Thich Nhat Hanh notes, "Food reveals our connection with the earth. Each bite contains the life of the sun and the earth. We can see and taste the whole universe in a piece of bread! Contemplating our food for a few seconds before eating and eating in mindfulness can bring us much happiness."

Conscious or Mindful Eating will change your life and the way you look at food going forward. Many people think that mindful eating is about eating slowly or about chewing your food for a long time because they don't know what mindful eating really means. Mindful Eating is much more than that. First is understanding that food is energy; it is fuel. Like anything else we need it to function and run. With the right fuel, you yield the right action.

Mindful Eating is maintaining an in-the-moment awareness of the food and drink you put into your body— being fully present and conscious while you are eating, observing rather than judging how the food makes you feel and the signals your body sends about taste, texture, and satisfaction, as well as identifying your body's true hunger and fullness signals. As a practice, mindful eating can bring us awareness of our own actions, thoughts, feelings, motivations, and insight into the roots of health and contentment. Learn how to do a mindful eating exercise or what is sometimes called eating meditation. When you are attuned to that important connection, you will provide your body with what it really needs to function. This is life altering.

Overall, the concept of Conscious Connections is important when your goal is to develop, deepen, and understand the value and importance of everyday occurrences such as mindful thinking; watching your words, emotions, and feelings; building strong relationships; consuming healthy foods, or whatever else you may want to focus on. You want to foster a healthy conscious connection with all things. The more we learn to become aware of the when, the what, and the why, we can use this knowledge and information to stay in control. We are then being mindful versus moving in a mindless existence. We become connected at a consciously high vibration.

THE S.P.I.C.E. OF LIFE

Conscious Connections Lessons Learned

Write your thoughts about these:

Does Conscious Connections fit in my life? If it does, where and how does it fit? If it doesn't, share your thoughts.

_____

_____

_____

_____

What is one Conscious Connections Practice that I will START now that will benefit my life's journey?

_____

_____

_____

_____

What is one Conscious Connections Practice that I will KEEP using because it has consistently worked for me?

_____

_____

_____

_____

What is one Conscious Connections Practice that I must STOP because it is not for my best and highest good?

_____

_____

THE S.P.I.C.E. OF LIFE

As I reflect on Conscious Connections, what do I believe?

As I reflect on Conscious Connections, what do I know?

What is my affirmation for my Conscious Connections? What is my overall goal?

What are some Divine Nurturing Words of comfort and peace for Conscious Connections?

THE S.P.I.C.E. OF LIFE

My Conscious Connections Story

Reflect on your life and think about your Conscious Connections Story. Did your childhood—or an experience—form or shape your conscious connections? If either did, how so? Use this space to write your Conscious Connections Story. You may consider your thoughts from "Conscious Connections: Lessons Learned" to help you write your story.

THE S.P.I.C.E. OF LIFE

THE S.P.I.C.E. OF LIFE

NOTES ON CONSCIOUS CONNECTIONS

Energy Management

ENERGY MANAGEMENT

All my life I thought I needed to get a handle on my time management. As you know, we all have 24 hours in a day; that is 1,440 minutes! I was encouraged to manage my time. I was told if I mastered it, I would have a productive and fulfilling life. Life comes at you, and if you do not manage it, it will manage you. No matter how hard I tried to manage my time, I didn't always feel productive or fulfilled. When I was in my 20s and early 30s as a single mother with a young child, I struggled. I was determined and persistent, yet still I struggled.

When you fall short, it affects your sense of being enough. You may not feel you have what it takes to succeed. I was dedicated to finishing my degree and obtaining a "good" job so that I could be a good mother and provider for my son. Throughout this time, I was going to school full-time during the day and working the night shift in the medical records department of a local hospital. I was earning a decent living while chasing my dreams. My days were easily 12-16 hours long. I felt perpetually exhausted. I found it difficult to fully engage with my child in the mornings, evenings, or at night, depending on what time I got home. I never wanted to depend on anyone; however, I must admit, I was blessed to have help with him. I had family members who supported me. I would drop him off somewhere in the mornings—at a babysitter as an infant, or at school when he was older. His grandfather would pick him up in the afternoons and take him to his home. During my days, I would go directly from school to work. I would be dead tired when I got off work, and I would pick my son up from my dad's place—often after midnight—and take him back home with me.

Although I was grateful for the help and routine, it also left me feeling guilty and dissatisfied. My son would often be asleep when I dropped him off in the early morning. He would be asleep when I brought him home at night. If he was awake when I picked him up at night, it was because he had not seen me all day. He would want to talk. He would ask me questions, and I would say, "Why do you want to know that?" One day, he said to me, "because I am curious, mama." I remember thinking, "curious"— when did he learn that word and where have I been? I was too tired and would often fall asleep. If I wasn't nodding off, I found myself telling him to just go to sleep, please. I slept poorly. I had no time to exercise. I seldom ate healthy meals; instead, I grabbed food to eat on the run. All of this was comical since I was well into my career as a nutrition professional. There I was learning about nutritious foods and healthy habits; yet, I did not devote time to practicing what I was learning. Seldom was I cooking healthy meals, let alone having any quality playtime with my child. Even on the weekends, I was studying, doing chores, and trying to balance my time management plan. A social life, what's that? When I look back and I think things over, I wish I had had knowledge of Energy Management. That is what I had sorely needed.

THE S.P.I.C.E. OF LIFE

I know that this experience is not uncommon. Most of us respond to rising demands in our lives in the form of longer hours, filled with stuff that we felt was important, which inevitably takes a toll on us physically, mentally, and emotionally. The core problem with working longer hours and chasing that dream is that time is a finite resource. You only have a limited amount of time each day, and that will never change. Just 24 hours. Only 1,440 minutes. That's it. That's what you get. That's what we each get!

How can Energy Management help? What exactly is Energy Management? It really opened my eyes when I was introduced to this concept by one of my mentors, Dr. Adolph Brown. When I began to research it, I found it to be intriguing and it made a lot of sense. It has been said that everything is Energy. Albert Einstein quipped, "Nothing happens until there is movement."

Dr. Wayne Dyer, author of *There's A Spiritual Solution To Every Problem,* says "Think of energy as vibrations and movement." We have within us the absolute ability to increase and enhance our energy field and vibrate into frequencies for everyday life. Dyer explains that in the slowest vibrations we have challenges, illness, and disharmony. Faster vibrations, is our positive consciousness, what some call the God consciousness.

I found there are many levels and deep references about personal energy. I want to be clear: I am not delving deep into the world of quantum physics and such; there are many others more qualified than I am to do that. In my research, I found that my willingness to shift my vibrational energy patterns has made all the difference in the trajectory of my life. I do this by refraining from giving my energy to what I don't believe in, what is not important or essential. I have put an end to things that are not for my best and highest good. When I fill that space and time with the highest of vibrations, it frees up so much more of my time, and it is more manageable. Energy impacts us at all times, and the frequency at which that energy moves determines our physical, mental, and spiritual health.

Energy Management is totally different from Time Management. It is essential to understand this difference. In "Manage your Energy, Not Your Time," Tony Schwartz and Catherine McCarthy explain that Energy Management comes from four main energy areas or fields in a person: *the Body, Emotions, Mind,* and *Spirit.* As I learned to focus on each energy area or energy field, I began to expand and regularly renewed myself. I established specific rituals, which are behaviors that are intentionally practiced. My goal remains to exhibit subconscious competence with Energy Management (you can find more information about Conscious Competence in Chapter Three). This is now an ongoing, permanent part of my life's journey.

To effectively re-energize myself, I realized that I needed to shift my emphasis from getting more out of myself to investing more in myself. When you choose to do this, you will get more out of yourself and more of the "right stuff" out of yourself. We usually focus on the actual time to manage the time we have each day. I know now that it is much more important to focus on managing my energy. Let me further emphasize that we must recharge, recognize the costs of energy-depleting behaviors, and then take responsibility for changing them, regardless of the circumstances we face.

Looking deeper into the difference between time management and personal energy management may provide clarity on this subject. Time Management is finite, which means it has limits and bounds. Time Management is about planning how much time you have in a day to do all you want, need, or desire. It's how you use this precious time each day to accomplish your planned activities that makes the difference. One important factor is that you do not have total control over your time. Any person, place, or thing can hijack your time at any moment.

Personal Energy Management is an awesome concept. It is about being aware of how much mental and physical energy you have throughout your day to do your planned activities. This is clearly where we get off track. Believe it or not, managing personal energy gives you more time. You may ask, "How can I have more time in those 24 hours I keep mentioning?" Well, regardless of your time management skills and how well you schedule your time, during those hours, managed energy will enable you to make better use of your time in your day, week, month, or year. It will help you feel the way you desire to feel. It can take away the thoughts of not being good or not being enough. You will end each day with a sense of accomplishment, despite how your day ends. It puts you in charge of your time. Throughout this book, we've talked about you having the power to choose. Choose today to take control of your life. Live by your agenda and not by the agendas of others. Where you have no control over your time, you definitely have total control over your actions, reactions, feelings, and thoughts. If your intention is to have a good day, you will have a good day, despite what happens that day.

When you do not have the personal energy to fulfill your commitments, things may not get done. There is a funny saying we all have heard: "If you want to make God laugh, make a plan." Although funny, it is giving us something very important to consider and understand. I stress that we have no control of what may happen in any given moment or any given day. The best-laid-out plans may just be wiped out due to something large or small that occurs—things you may not have thought about ... like a pandemic. Yep, that is a perfect example, we are living it right now. As I write this book, the world is in the middle of a pandemic. We had no control over this. Well, we have mini-pandemics frequently in our daily lives. We can only control how we respond to them. Our perfectly planned life and time can be completely altered by something we would not or could not have thought of or planned for. Now that we have experienced it, we know what we need to do to plan for it going forward. Life will always give us unexpected surprises.

However, this could and often does manifest as a more simple scenario such as I plan to arrive at work by 8:00 am and then I run into a major car accident on the road. Your personal Energy Management is working from within you and not from outside. This is something we can control. Even though you will still make it to work, your day may or may not be altered. This will be based on your use of your energy management consciousness versus your time management consciousness. Our vibrations and conscious temperament may either cause you to not be fully present or move with ease into your day. After all, it was not your fault. Your brain may be a little foggy, and your body will either be tense with stress or slouchy based on how you are feeling. You'll arrive complaining and fussing, and all that comes along with that level of awareness. That stuff is time-consuming. When you combine managing your personal energy with managing your time, you will become happier, fully present in the conversation, and effective. Just get to work and keep it moving. In other words, when managing your personal energy, nothing can disturb your peace of mind. In the midst of chaos, I have often been asked, "How can you stay so calm?" It is embedded within me. My personal energy is calmness.

Let's briefly look into the four Energy fields: The Body, Emotions, Mind, and Spirit.

The Body: Physical Energy

This refers to our functional and physical energy. This is super important. In the *Personal Growth and Development* chapter, I wrote about the importance of taking care of our bodies. We know that inadequate nutrition, limited movement, and poor sleep, rest, and hydration all diminish our basic energy levels. We know that these also hamper the ability to manage our emotions and focus our attention. Because of the demands in our lives, many of us lack ways to consistently practice these healthy behaviors. The truth is, we cannot manage our lives properly without the knowledge and understanding of how our bodies work for us. By now you know my mantra, "Awareness Builds Clarity," is appropriate to share. The more we seek to know, the more we will see and understand that this is all in our hands and under our control. Yes, there may be some things that are not completely in our control. Such things might be genetic, heredity, or present in others. Ultimately, this is about your agency and advocacy. It's about you exercising the power to change most things that are not working for you.

When focusing on your BODY, there are helpful strategies and rituals for building and renewing physical energy. Some of us are significantly overweight, eat poorly, lack a regular exercise routine, work long hours, and typically sleep no more than five hours a night. It is as simple as knowing your energy and then seeking balance. This is the ultimate way to maintain your weight. Your energy intake (food) versus your energy expenditure is one key factor in your overall energy balance. The art of learning how to manage those two concepts can unlock your optimum desired body weight.

Another key strategy in physical energy management is to take brief but regular breaks at specific intervals throughout the workday. Our bodies slowly move from a high-energy state into a peaceful, thoughtful realm. Toward the end of each cycle, the body begins to crave a period of recovery. The signals include physical restlessness, yawning, hunger, and difficulty concentrating, but many of us ignore them and keep going. What happens next? Our energy reservoir—our remaining capacity—burns down as the day wears on. Intermittent breaks for renewal have been found to result in higher and more sustainable performance. It will clear up mental blocks and periods when we feel stuck. Taking a break clears the blockage and frees your thought process. The length of renewal is less important than the quality. It is possible to get a great deal of recovery in a short time—as little as several minutes—if it involves a ritual that allows you to disengage from work and truly shift directions, if only for a moment. That little shift could range from getting up to talk to someone about something other than work, to listening to music, to walking up and down stairs in an office building—anything not work-related. Take those moments. How can that free up time? Instead of sitting stuck on something for an hour or more, a quick 10-minute mental break can allow your mental flow to open up and could save you 45 minutes.

The Emotions: Quality of Energy

Taking more control of our emotions can improve the quality of our energy, regardless of the external pressures we face. To do this, we first must become more aware of how we feel throughout the day and of the impact these emotions may be having on our effectiveness (There is that word again! Remember "Awareness Builds Clarity"!). We tend to perform our best when we are feeling positive energy. I know that is true for me, and I am sure you would agree: Positive energy puts me in a zone of high vibrations; it's the Zone of Awesomeness!

It's most important to have the intention that every day is a "good day"! Claim it first thing in the morning. No matter what you know is in store for you this day, you still affirm, as Dr. Adolph Brown says, "Today is going to be a Good Day." You must claim this before you get your day started. One simple but powerful ritual for defusing negative emotions is as simple as breathing. Deep abdominal breathing is one way to do that: breathe deeply through our nose counting to five, then hold your breath for a count of five, and then exhale slowly for a count of five. Repeat two more times. This induces relaxation and recovery.

Conscious, mindful breathing is something I do every day. When you breathe consciously, you are embracing the "Present." Think about it. You cannot breathe from yesterday and you cannot breathe for tomorrow. You can only breathe right NOW, in the moment. This is your verification of the here and now. This is what brings me to what I call my "GOD Center." I make sure I do this first thing in the morning and often two to three times a day. It is also great to do when you are feeling anxious, stressed, or blocked. This has become such a subconscious tool that my body will immediately start this when it feels stress coming on. I am not even aware until I find myself there. There have been occasions when I don't even realize it is happening. I was once at a work-related meeting and I stepped out to take a disturbing call from my boss. When I returned to the meeting, after a few minutes of sitting and re-engaging in the meeting, calmly listening, I thought, the person sitting next to me asked me if I was ok. I replied, "Yes. Why do you ask?" She explained I was breathing so deeply. I had not even realized it, but my body had gone into a subconscious defense mechanism. My peace will not be moved.

Other rituals may help in keeping you on an even keel, include singing or humming uplifting or spiritual songs, saying a special prayer, or reading a bible verse that resonates with you. Powerful ritual that creates positive emotions in expressing appreciation to others, a practice that seems to be as beneficial to the giver as to the receiver, can take the form of a handwritten note, an email, a phone call, or a pleasant conversation—and the more detailed and specific, the higher the impact. As with all rituals, setting aside a particular time to do it vastly increases the chances of success. Therefore, setting time aside to do those things such as listening to music, prayer work, and meditation works beautifully when taming and controlling our emotions.

People can foster positive emotions by learning to change the stories they tell themselves and others about the events in their lives. This is something I had pretty bad when I was younger. I had an early tragedy in my life. I often told the stories time after time, which kept my emotions in flames. It was so very sad that it kept me in a state of sadness. In the chapter on *Conscious Connections* we explored how words, thoughts, and feelings dictate your life and circumstances. Please believe and know that. If you get nothing else from these readings, know how powerful your thoughts are. I once lived as a sad, pathetic person. I was a sob storyteller. Often, people in conflict cast themselves in the role of victim, blaming others or external circumstances for their problems. Becoming aware of the difference between the facts in a given situation and the way we interpret those facts can be powerful in itself. It's been a revelation for many of the people I worked with to discover they have a choice about how to view a given event and to recognize how powerfully the story they tell influences the emotions they feel. I encourage individuals to tell the most hopeful and personally empowering story possible in any given situation without denying or minimizing the facts. I mean it is just a matter of turning it around for your best and highest good. You may not see that at first, but soon you will. Find the diamond in your story and let it shine. "Keep your head to the sky" as Earth Wind and Fire powerfully sing!

The Mind: Focus of Energy

Are you one of those people who pride yourself on being a multitasker? That was me, for sure. Yeah, we think we are masters of juggling, but it actually undermines us. Distractions are costly: A temporary shift in attention from one task to another—stopping to answer an e-mail or take a phone call, for instance. This practice increases the amount of time necessary to finish the primary task. It's far more efficient to fully focus for 90-120 minutes, take a true break, and then fully focus on the next activity. It is okay to stay focused and not answer that call, for instance. You may feel you are multitasking, but in actuality, one activity is being neglected—either the person you are half listening to or the task on which you are now not fully focusing. Once people see how much they struggle to concentrate, they can create rituals to reduce the relentless interruptions that technology has introduced in their lives.

One of the best things I finally did, but was one of the hardest to master, was to eliminate distractions. People had to make appointments or be announced before they could come into my office, even my good friends who often thought they had carte blanche—complete freedom to just walk in my office when they felt like it. And even though people made jokes and would say I was being high and mighty, they eventually learned to respect me for it. Because when I did meet with them I could, and I did give them my full undivided attention and responded effectively, rather than half way listening or rushing them away. It really worked. You and your time are valuable and you're not at everyone's beckon call. It was something I had to learn. These are sure ways that you can keep a clear mind. You can get a lot done with a clear mind, right? And your time is not hijacked.

The Human Spirit: Energy of Meaning and Purpose

People tap into the energy of the human spirit when their everyday work and activities are consistent with what they value most and with what gives them a sense of meaning and purpose. If the work they're doing really matters to them, they typically feel more positive energy, focus better, and demonstrate greater perseverance. Unfortunately, the high demands and fast pace of life don't leave much time to pay attention to these issues, and many people don't even recognize meaning and purpose as potential sources of energy. Just think, when we experience the value of what we are doing, we then start to see that being attentive to our own deeper needs dramatically influences the effectiveness and satisfaction of our life.

To access the energy of the human spirit, people need to clarify priorities and establish accompanying rituals in three categories: (1) doing what they do best and enjoy most at work or play; (2) consciously allocating time and energy to the areas of their lives—work, family, health, service to others etc.—whatever they deem most important; and (3) living their core values in their daily behaviors.

What you do best: When you're attempting to discover what you do best and what you enjoy most, it's important to realize that these two things aren't necessarily mutually inclusive. You may get lots of positive feedback about something you're very good at, but you truly do not enjoy it. Conversely, you can love doing something but have no gift for it, so achieving success requires much more energy than it makes sense to invest. An example I'd like to share here is an experience that really changed the trajectory of my life and my work. I attended training where there was an activity that was conducted where we had to think about and write down "Our God Given Gifts and Talents" (Head, Heart and Hands/Feet). It was funny, because it was something I had never really taken the time to think about. What I found out was life-affirming and heart-chattering for me. My Head talent and my Heart talent were in direct conflict. I literally finally understood why I felt so off balance. I cried because I knew I was in the wrong line of work and that is why I was so unhappy. You see, my head talent was in management-leadership-supervisor mode, and my heart was to nurture, mentor, love, support, and uplift people. As a leader, I couldn't really care why someone would not come to work, for example; yet, my heart did care and I did not want to discipline them for being off work so much. I felt people were people and they were good people and those with challenges just needed support and assistance. It was awful and made my job difficult. However, I had to handle it, and often felt bad because either the person had to get written up or terminated. If I did not handle the situation, I felt bad for the stress it put on the other staff. It was hard on those who had to take up the slack due to the person's frequent absence. Also, if I didn't handle it, I felt like an inadequate manager. My spirit energy was not at rest. That had to change and it did. I had to find a way to merge the two so that my spirit was at peace. Otherwise, I needed to get out of the field of work.

Devoting time and energy: When doing this consciously to what's important to you, there is often a similar divide between what people say is important and what they actually do. Rituals can help close this gap. We may realize that devoting time to moments and experiences with family is what matters most; however, such things get squeezed out of the day more often than we would like. You can consider instituting a ritual in which you switch off or disconnect from work for at least three hours every evening when you get home. This would help you focus uninterrupted time on family. This one—I know—is challenging and I also know that lost time can never be replaced. Find a solution to invest the time. You'll feel better for it; trust me.

Living core values: Practicing your core values in your everyday behavior is a challenge for many as well. Most people are living at such a furious pace that they rarely stop to ask themselves what they stand for and who they want to be. As a consequence, they let external demands dictate their actions.

Do not attempt to define your values, because the results are usually too predictable. Instead, seek to uncover them, in part by asking questions that are inadvertently revealing, such as, "What are the qualities that you find most off-putting when you see them in others?" By describing what they dislike, people unintentionally divulge what they like. If you are very offended by stinginess, for example, generosity is probably one of your key values. If you are especially put off by rudeness in others, it's likely that consideration is a high value for you. As in the other categories, establishing rituals can help bridge the gap between the values you aspire to and how you currently behave. Keep in mind you are not judging others; you are tapping into who you are. If you discover that consideration is a key value, but you are perpetually late for meetings, the ritual might be to end the meetings you run five minutes earlier than usual and intentionally show up five minutes early for the meeting that follows. Being habitually late is a good one. Yes, we all are late from time to time. But those of you—and you know who you are—who find yourself always late, this one for you. NO one is always anything, unless you are not concerned about this trait. A friend of mine told me that she was admonished once for being late. The person told her she was inconsiderate. I know and understand you may have not looked at it this way. Ultimately, she is showing up as inconsiderate of others. How are you showing up in life? Are you showing up in a way you don't like? And if that is not the way you want to show up, make this a priority to change. You can, if you care to.

Addressing these three categories helps people go a long way toward achieving a greater sense of alignment, satisfaction, and well-being in all aspects of their lives. Those feelings are a source of positive energy in their own right and reinforce people's desires to persist at rituals in other energy dimensions as well.

So, what happens when you combine personal energy and time management?

When you use personal energy and time management, you'd be surprised how much more time you'll have to do more. You spend less time dealing with emotions because you've built in space to respond to life. You become more effective, efficient, and accomplished. You discover your Personal Energy and how focusing on the energy your family gives you can fuel you throughout the day. You discover that time doesn't matter as much because your personal energy begins to dictate how you'll spend your time.

I recommend you take a Personal Energy Assessment. I've included a sample assessment in the Extra Ingredients section. The assessment is adapted from *Manage Your Energy, Not Your Time* by Schwartz and McCarthy for your consideration. The assessment includes questions in each energy dimension—body, emotions, mind, and spirit. The questions can help you highlight your greatest energy deficits and raise your awareness about how certain areas in your life will influence your energy levels. The Personal Energy Assessment will direct you to some of the areas you can enhance toward building a better and fulfilling life. Once you are aware of where and how your energy is being depleted or lacking, you become clear and possibly determine if you are in or headed towards a personal energy crisis. You'll then know what areas to focus on and tackle, and then make whatever personal steps are needed for your highest and best good.

Energy Management Strategies

Twenty-six strategies (A to Z) to ignite, activate, and achieve Energy management; integrate some or all of these in your daily life, or create your own. See how they make a difference, if done routinely.

1. **A**lways schedule time for mind, body and soul work
2. **B**reak your days into micro tasks
3. **C**reate a *Peaks and Valleys* journal
4. **D**rinking water can boost your energy
5. **E**xercise and movement activates your energy for the day
6. **F**uel the body and include plant-based foods
7. **G**ive dedicated time to your loved ones
8. **H**aving ME time! It's your right!
9. **I**dentify and own your true feelings
10. **J**oy, joy, joy, deep in your soul, tap into it

11. **K**eep your thoughts in the balcony, the upper room
12. **L**ove yourself as God loves you
13. **M**otivations—Find what moves you
14. **N**otice and avoid energy drainers
15. **O**vercome all obstacles by being self aware and conscious of your thoughts
16. **P**rioritize your own time before someone else does
17. **Q**uality time is essential
18. **R**ejoice in your daily wins, the small and large wins
19. **S**tay focused and set your daily intentions
20. **T**ake charge of your day
21. **U**nderstand you can do all things, just not all at the same time
22. **V**isualize your Life Light
23. **W**alk daily—simply move as often as you can
24. **X** out all the unwanted noise in your head or unplug for an hour
25. **Y**ield to what your mind and body are telling you
26. **Z**ero in on your breathing which represents the present and peace

THE S.P.I.C.E. OF LIFE

Energy Management Lessons Learned

Write your thoughts about these:

Does Energy Management fit in my life? If it does, where and how does it fit? If it doesn't, share your thoughts.

_____

_____

_____

_____

What is one Energy Management Practice that I will START now that will benefit my life's journey?

_____

_____

_____

_____

What is one Energy Management Practice that I will KEEP using because it has consistently worked for me?

_____

_____

_____

_____

What is one Energy Management Practice that I must STOP because it is not for my best and highest good?

_____

_____

_____

THE S.P.I.C.E. OF LIFE

As I reflect on Energy Management, what do I believe?

As I reflect on Energy Management, what do I know?

What is my affirmation for my Energy Management? What is my overall goal?

What are some Divine Nurturing Words of comfort and peace for Energy Management?

THE S.P.I.C.E. OF LIFE

My Energy Management Story

Reflect on your life and think about your Energy Management Story. Did your childhood—or an experience—form or shape your energy management? If either did, how so? Use this space to write your Energy Management Story. You may consider your thoughts from "Energy Management: Lessons Learned" to help you write your story.

THE S.P.I.C.E. OF LIFE

THE S.P.I.C.E. OF LIFE

NOTES ON ENERGY MANAGEMENT

Final Warning

FINAL WARNING

We all have tough times and breakdowns throughout our lives. When we look back; however, we can see that life has been good. As Rev. Paul Jones sings,

> *I've had some good days, I've had some hills to climb,*
> *But when I look around, And I think things over,*
> *All of my good days, Outweigh my bad days, I won't*
> *complain.*

We have as us, before us, and around us the power and the tools God placed within us to survive all things.

When you look at where you are today, you have made it through. You've made it through whatever you were going through or growing through. You have persevered. You were resilient and overcame. You survived. You are thriving. Many of you are flourishing at your highest level on your path of self-realization. You have made the ultimate breakthrough—To know ThySelf and love ThySelf so you can fully love others.

The journey to transformation is not something you do alone. Not at all. You have the people, tools, and the indwelling Presence of a Higher Power. Your path is your path, and you are never alone. Whether you call this presence God, Spirit, Jesus, Higher Power, The Law, Divine Intelligence, Eternal Creator, The Buddha, Angels, or the Ancestors, this presence is here for you. Even those living around you today—whether they are parents, aunts, uncles, grandparents, godparents, fictive kin, friends, and even strangers—are present and are here for you. They walk before us, guiding our way. They walk beside and with us, supporting us. They walk behind us, giving us that nudge or push we may need at the right moment to move us forward. Most importantly and impactful are the times when life seems too hard and we feel we cannot make it through; and, yet, we do because they are tarrying with us and carrying us over.

I know you can be guided through change with the attributes, tips, and suggestions in this book or through your own creative ideas. When you apply what is already within you or at your fingertips, you will make this a personal growth process. Using your internal wisdom, you will make the shifts and changes that set you free. You have the power to shake free of whatever is holding you back. Let those old thoughts go—the ones that are holding you hostage. The one thing we do have control of is our thoughts, our mindset. Change it, transform it, shift it. Just do it!

I started this book journey with "On a Clear Day (You Can See Forever)," a song by Alan Lerner that my mother used to sing. At the time I did not know the real meaning of these words and how they would play such an integral role in my life's existence:

On a clear day
Rise and look around you
And you'll see who you are.

THE S.P.I.C.E. OF LIFE

On a clear day
How it will astound you
That the glow of your being outshines ev'ry star.

My motto in life is *Awareness Builds Clarity* ^{TM}. I know that it is my awareness and acceptance of God's Presence that makes my words, thoughts, and feelings effective and thus provides a clear path. Then and only then will your answers come. Through these lenses, Seek to be clear. Seek to understand the world around you, how to navigate in this world. Seek to know the real you, the true you. I have found that when I take the time and keep my eyes open to see my own truth, it really does not matter what others think or say. That is their business, should they choose to venture into my world instead of focusing on their own. Stop trying to explain or seek approval from others about your choices and your personal business.

I have found that life teaches us and warns us time and time again. Maybe symbolically or sometimes blatantly, right in our faces, like when I was let go from my job. It is always right in front of me. Often we are just blind to the truth. I now know and accept the fact that during my life I did more for others than I did for myself. I think I was made that way. I was raised by women who did for others and nurtured others, who were kind to others. That is what I saw. They were "Doing" women. And doing some of the things I did made me feel good, and I felt I was living my purpose. Although this may have been my calling or purpose, being true and honest with myself was needed to complete my life journey. I needed to learn how to just

"Be." I am keeping my consciousness right and learning to embrace my Truths and "Be" my authentic self.

Often we miss or ignore the warning signs. These signs are our "Blessings in Disguise." The message in these writings brings home the fact that we have the power, the choice, the abilities, the resilience, and the perseverance—you name it—to transform our lives. Making small shifts, changing our thoughts and our minds, watching our words, and living by our own intentions and not others, are keys to our peace of mind. Owning your awesomeness, embracing the wonderful individualized expressions that you are, to not be ashamed to know who you are, regardless of what you think others may think, to be fearless and flawless in the eyes of your maker, these are your birthright!

I have moved through this life and may have not always been in my right environment, either physically, mentally, or spiritually; however, I believe wherever I am, I am meant to be right there at that moment. I have learned to take a breath, take a moment, and take it all in addressing these questions:

> *Why am I here?*
> *What is my lesson?*
> *What are my blessings in this?*
> *What good does this have for my life?*

Sometimes you have to dig deep for the answers, but they will come. Align your subconscious mind with your conscious mind; the answers are revealed.

THE S.P.I.C.E. OF LIFE

Living your best life means making sure that you are covered and anchored in your spirituality; taking pride in your personal development and continued growth; deeply diving into an introspective look at yourself, within yourself, and around yourself; mindfully making conscious connections with all of life; and fully embracing the concept of energy management. This is what many call self-care, I call God-Care. I trust you are inspired, motivated, and excited about continuing your journey—no matter where you are at this point in your life—to be the best individual you are ordained to be.

Best wishes and happy sojourning to your transformative life.

NOTES ON FINAL WARNING

THE S.P.I.C.E. OF LIFE

Extra Ingredients

THE S.P.I.C.E. OF LIFE

EXTRA INGREDIENT:
The SPICE of Life Wheel ™ Menu of Possibilities

The SPICE of Life Wheel ™ has two essential aspects. The first essential aspect is your circumference. It is never divided or sliced. It cements and holds us together. It is a must for your life. While the circumference or the outer is changeless, the inner is about how you devote yourself to what makes life fulfilling. It will change as you slice and divide things to your desire. This is where you determine how much time and energy you will devote to certain areas of your life. What comes to mind for these areas:

- Faith and Spirituality
- Physical Environment and Community
- Fun and Recreation
- Family and Friends
- Romance and Relationship
- Personal Growth
- Finances
- Fitness
- Education and Career
- Business and Entrepreneurship
- Mental and Physical Well-Being

Use *The SPICE of Life Wheels* on the following pages to brainstorm your specific areas of focus—the inward stuff.

THE S.P.I.C.E. OF LIFE

SPIRITUALITY
PERSONAL GROWTH AND DEVELOPMENT
INTROSPECTION
CONSCIOUS CONNECTIONS
ENERGY MANAGEMENT

EXTRA INGREDIENT:
My Five Keys to a Transformative Life

THE FIRST KEY: *Always Lead From Your Heart*

My nephew, Akhenaten Daaood, is a personal trainer. I visited him one week in Northern California. I asked him to work with me on the proper daily exercises for someone my age. He took his 60+ year old auntie through a rigorous set of exercises; well, they were rigorous for me but probably not really that hard. Out of all of the things he taught me that day, little does he know, there was one message that enlightened me and that I took with me from that day on. I still live by this to this day. While we were going through proper posture techniques, he had me stand up straight, arms at my side, stomach and core in and chest out. He then instructed me to bring my arms straight out to each side, like I was about to fly. From this position I raised my arm straight up toward the sky, where my hand touched over my head. At this point, keeping my body aligned, bringing my arms back down to my side I ended up in what is called a neural spine position. In this ultimate posture position, he then said the most profound words to me. "Auntie, when you are in this posture you are Leading Life with your Heart." Now when I find myself with poor posture, I immediately straighten up. I want to always lead with my Heart. Those I have shared with may hear me say, when I see people slouching or holding their body or head down, "Hey, LEAD WITH YOUR HEART." That immediately makes them do two things: correct their posture and open up their hearts. I suggest that everything you do, every day, lead with your heart, this equates to leading Life with Love.

THE SECOND KEY: *Believe and Have Faith – The Faith of a Mustard Seed*

All things begin as a seed, planted in our minds and consciousness, or in the ground. All things come from this path. We have all heard Matthew 17:20: "Because you have so little faith. Truly I tell you, if you have faith like a grain of mustard seed, you can say to this mountain, 'Move from here to there,' and it will move. Nothing will be impossible for you." Often our perspectives are shaped by outside forces on television, social media, or just what we experience in our environments. This can give a false sense of belief, and if we see the worse we tend to think the worse. Regardless of where we are in life, our faith matters. The lack of faith can sabotage our actions and intentions. The faith that knows the sun will come up each day, flowers will bloom, birds will sing, and trees will grow are things we don't worry about at night. If we put $100 in the bank, we do not check every day to see if it is still there. Why? Because we have faith and we know it will be there when we go back. Live in the action step of faith, it is meant to grow. Have Faith in all things! Just like a mustard seed! Plant the seeds you want to see grow in your life.

THE S.P.I.C.E. OF LIFE

THE THIRD KEY: *Seek Your Sun, It Is Always There, Even Behind the Clouds*

The light will pull you towards it, just like living plants seek sunlight. Often we are in a safe and comfortable place, yet we feel the pull. We know we have the potential to do and be more. It is not just to survive—though surviving is good—but to grow and glow. We must branch out to the right environment—the right soil —to allow our full potential to bloom. The sky's the limit.

THE FOURTH KEY: *Shift Your Environment, Shift Your Thoughts, Shift Your Mindset, And Shift Your Words Constantly*

This is a plant that my dear Aunt Linda and Uncle Charles Gage purchased years and years ago (Image A). Its growth was stunted in this spot and this container. It was beginning to thrive; yet, it seemed to be struggling. It needed more space to do so. My Aunt decided to move the pot to a different location. She moved the plant to the side of the garage. Twenty years later, I visited town and my aunt had since transitioned. My uncle showed me what happened to the plant. I could not believe the plant had grown into a tree. Just as my aunt knew to be the truth, once the plant was relocated, it had what it needed and it grew exponentially into its ultimate potential. It became a full-grown tree with abundant leaves stretching towards the SUN (Image B). It found the right environment and soil needed to flourish. I encourage you to have faith to shift your environment, thoughts, mindset, and your words to inhabit the spaces and places to experience your full potential. When you do so, you are not leaving your roots—you are honoring them.

  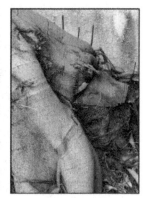

Image A   *Image B*   *Image C*

THE FIFTH KEY: *Honor Your Roots*

As my uncle drew me even closer to the tree, I made another discovery. The original pot that contained—and even restrained—the plant from so many years ago was still there. Somehow when the plant became a tree it grew and grew around and through the pot (Image C). It was embedded in the tree! Here is the beautifully symbolic and important message: no matter where we may go, we are never far from our roots. We must honor who and whose we are and we must honor our origins and our pasts. The original container is still very much connected to the plant that has become a tree. In truth, those who come before us never leave us. They are just as much a part of us now as they were then. They get us started, and let us go and grow on our own, thus allowing us to reach our full potential.

Take a few moments to reflect on *My Five Keys to a Transformative Life*. Which key speaks to you the most? Which key gives you pause? Write what comes to mind below and then take the next few days to thoughtfully focus on these two keys.

THE S.P.I.C.E. OF LIFE

EXTRA INGREDIENT:
Personal Energy Assessment

Please check the statements below that are true for you.

BODY
☐ I regularly get at least seven or eight hours of sleep.

☐ I work out enough (i.e., cardio training 3+ times and strength training 1+ time a week).

☐ I take regular breaks each day to renew and recharge.

☐ I don't allow myself to get stretched too thin.

☐ I eat foods that support physical health and well-being.

EMOTIONS
☐ I do not find myself feeling irritable or anxious at work, especially when work is demanding.

☐ I have enough time with loved ones, and when I'm with them, I'm fully present and I know they can tell.

☐ I have time for the activities that I most deeply enjoy.

☐ I stop frequently enough to express my appreciation to others or to savor my accomplishments and blessings.

☐ I feel my time is purposeful. I work on my agenda and other agendas. And this pleases me.

MIND
☐ I am successful at focusing on one thing at a time. I am not easily distracted during the day, especially by email or constant interruptions.

THE S.P.I.C.E. OF LIFE

☐ I spend much of my day focusing on activities with longer term value and high leverage, rather than reacting to immediate crises and demands.

☐ I make enough time for reflection, strategizing, and creative thinking.

☐ I do not work in the evenings or on weekends, and I usually take an email-free vacation.

☐ I appropriately disconnect from work or whatever project I am working on.

SPIRIT

☐ I devote time at work doing what I do best and enjoy most.

☐ There aren't significant gaps between what I say is most important and how I actually allocate time and energy.

☐ My decisions in life are more often influence by a strong, clear sense of my own purpose, rather than by external demands.

☐ I invest time and energy in making a positive difference to others or to the world.

☐ I pray or meditate daily.

Reflect on the four areas (Body, Emotions, Mind, Spirit):

- Where do you have all five boxes checked?
- Where do you have less than three boxes checked?
- Where might you focus your attention over the next 30 days to achieve a breakthrough?

EXTRA INGREDIENT:
Getting Your Book Written and Published

As a bonus feature, if you write responses to each of the chapter reflections you will have written your own book! Now you're wondering, "So what?" Great question! Why not take what you have written and get it published! Depending on what you have written and your feelings about it, you can use any of the following tips to get your book written and published.

1. WRITING PARTNER: Find a writing coach or an accountability partner to support you in getting your book finished.
2. COPY EDITOR: Hire a copy editor to read your draft book to ensure it flows and makes sense. They will read what you have written and offer helpful suggestions for improvement.
3. PUBLISHER: Think about how you will publish your book; choose the way that makes the most sense for you and your book:
   - *Traditional trade publishing* gives us the books we see in local booksellers and national chain bookstores. Their writers don't pay to get published.
   - *Boutique press publishing* focuses on a niche market and is usually done by small publishing houses. Their writers may or may not pay to get published.

- *Independent publishing* is also known as self-publishing. These writers pay for everything related to publishing their books.

I've had the idea for this book since 2017—and ideas for other books for over 30 years. If you're like me, you get ideas all the time. I decided to just do it and not allow anything to get in my way. First, I imagined what my book would look like on the shelf in my favorite bookstore. Then I just started writing about my life. Soon, I participated in a writing workshop. It helped me to get more thoughts on paper. I found myself looking at books differently—what did I like about those I saw? What was missing? What could I add? Not long after, I participated in a Writing Mastermind group. That's when I really got focused on the topic of this book. We met a couple of times a month to help each other think about our writing and we also sat down and wrote! Eventually, I hired a writing coach to work with me one-on-one to publish the book you're now holding in your hands.

If you have realized your dream of writing your first book as a result of reading this book, I applaud you and I celebrate with you! I would love to hear about your success regardless of the topic, size, or purpose of your book. Please go to my website (www.dkeyingredient.com) and drop me a note to let me know. You can even send "I did it!" and keep it moving! Now, before you publish your book, I'd be honored to write an Advance Praise comment about your relentlessness, persistence, and drive. Visit my website and let me know.

INDEX

ABOUT THE AUTHOR

DEBRA L. KEYES is the founder of DKeyingredient Consultants LLC (DKC). As Chief Consultant of DKC, she harnesses over four decades of experience and craft knowledge to support individuals and organizations with personal, spiritual, and professional growth and development.

A native of Los Angeles, California, her career includes service to hospitals, community clinics, universities, and private and non-profit organizations, where she successfully orchestrated major program changes and enhancements to improve metrics and outcomes. She led efforts with various programs—including Los Angeles-based Federally Qualified Community Health Centers—as a federal, state, local, and private grants administrator. She served as the Department Head for Maternal and Child Health Programs and Agency Director for the Special Supplemental Nutrition Program for Women, Infants, and Children (WIC). As a State WIC Director, she provided overall strategic oversight and overall team responsibility to ensure compliance with federal regulations.

A registered and licensed dietitian, she is a multifaceted, intersectional woman of faith and tenacity who deftly blends her knowledge of mindfulness, health, and wellness with her experience as a Licensed Spiritual Practitioner (Professional Practitioner Emeritus status) with the Center for Spiritual Living (formerly, Church of Religious Science). Her practice as a spiritual life coach is informed and guided by her tutelage with Dr. Daniel L. Morgan, Rev. Nirvana

Gayle, Rev. Juanita Dunn, and Bishop Dr. Barbara Lewis King.

A "Real Talk" presenter, she uses humor and wit to share hard-to-hear truths that lead to profound transformations. She emphasizes positive health strategies for all with a special focus on women in corporate and nonprofit leadership. While her lessons spring from her education and career, she has found her personal life story to be most impactful with her clients. Indeed, she notes, *Awareness Builds Clarity* ™ for each of us. She serves her profession as faculty with the National WIC Association Leadership Academy and she is an active member of Hillside International Truth Center. She is a proud member of Dr. Adolph Brown's Doc and Friends—Speakers Bureau, Ordinary People with Extraordinary Messages.

Although she has received several accolades throughout her journey, she is most appreciative of being honored by WEN (Women Empowerment Network) with its Diamond Award For An Extraordinary Women for her Commitment to Empower and Inspire Others to Greatness.

SPEAKING AND CONSULTING

Debra L. Keyes is available for speaking engagements, coaching, and training. For more information, contact:

Dkeyingredient.com
dkeyingredient@gmail.com
678-667-3301